Whispers
from a
Lebanese
Kitchen

A family's treasured recipes

Nouha Taouk

From left: Hind, Joumana, Citi Leila, Therese and Rosa.

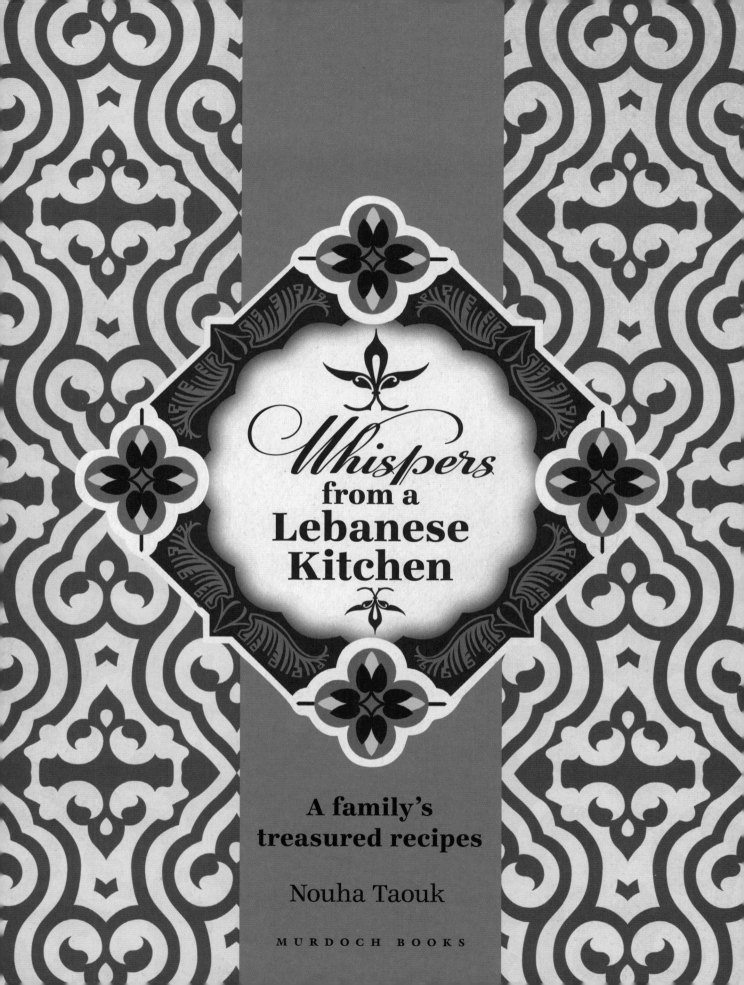

Whispers from a Lebanese Kitchen

A family's treasured recipes

Nouha Taouk

MURDOCH BOOKS

Contents

The Family Story

A mortar and a pestle were the first utensils given to me so I could contribute to one of our family cook-offs. It happened in Citi (grandmother) Leila's kitchen when I was about five years old. Citi must have seen me standing there looking desperate to join in with the women as they chopped, processed, stirred and laughed their way through the production of a formidable selection of tantalising dishes. Citi leaned towards me and handed me my tools, as if it was part of an initiation. Inside the mortar were two bulbs of garlic sprinkled with a little salt. 'Here you go my sweetheart, it's time to make your favourite,' she said. 'You want me to make taratoor?' I responded in a high-pitched voice that betrayed my shock and delight. 'Just like I have taught you,' she continued, and then gave me a wink along with some further encouragement: 'With your wonderful hands I know that you will make it taste better.' She then sat me at the kitchen table and sent me on my garlic-sauce-making way. I remember feeling a bit overwhelmed but eager to do well and I was proud when I successfully made this dish—one that requires determination and brute strength to make it well. I did my best to impress Citi, carefully drizzling in the oil and then the lemon juice while continuing to stir, not stopping until the mixture had become a thick fluffy sauce. The experience was rewarding, and from then on I began to develop an appreciation of food and cooking.

Every family has their story—mine is best told through food. As the first-born Australian–Lebanese girl of around one-hundred grandchildren, I have always felt the need to savour our family recipes, afraid that they may lose their flavour with time. They carry with them priceless stories and memories from the women who have shaped my understanding and appreciation of our culture and femininity, and of course our culinary traditions. Citi Leila and her daughters—my mother Joumana and my aunties Hind, Rosa and Therese—are the dynamic forces behind everything that our family stands for.

Citi is usually found hidden in the dense vegetation of her suburban backyard. Her garden, filled with vegetables of all kinds, is a vital part of her recipes. It is her pride and joy; her love affair, really. She spends most of her days planting, nurturing and reaping the rewards of a lush garden that occupies nearly half her backyard.

At seventy-three years of age, Citi is tall with a solid frame. Her short and wiry grey hair contrasts with her little mouse-like nose, almond-shaped green eyes and refined cheekbones. She has raised seven children almost single-handedly, and assisted with raising twenty-seven of her grandchildren. Just as her garden serves her, she is the nourishment and foundation of our family.

Citi's Australian journey began in the late 1970s, when Lebanon was on the brink of civil war. She and her five children boarded a plane bound for Sydney, leaving behind the rural life of Becharee, a village situated 1400 metres above sea level in the centre of Lebanon's largest mountain range, taking up residence with her husband, Gidi, a man who they had not seen for ten years.

Citi and Gidi had made huge sacrifices, living in different parts of the world for ten years. Back in Becharee, Citi juggled cultivating the crops that sustained them and raising six children under the age of ten. When Gidi decided to leave his beloved Lebanon behind, he was following his instinct. He could feel that something negative was in the air. So he headed to Sydney where he worked in factories to

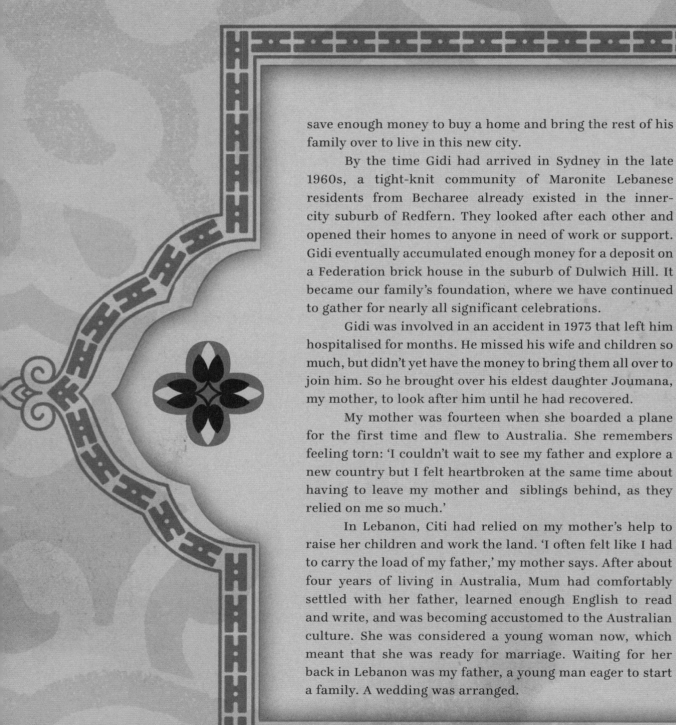

save enough money to buy a home and bring the rest of his family over to live in this new city.

By the time Gidi had arrived in Sydney in the late 1960s, a tight-knit community of Maronite Lebanese residents from Becharee already existed in the inner-city suburb of Redfern. They looked after each other and opened their homes to anyone in need of work or support. Gidi eventually accumulated enough money for a deposit on a Federation brick house in the suburb of Dulwich Hill. It became our family's foundation, where we have continued to gather for nearly all significant celebrations.

Gidi was involved in an accident in 1973 that left him hospitalised for months. He missed his wife and children so much, but didn't yet have the money to bring them all over to join him. So he brought over his eldest daughter Joumana, my mother, to look after him until he had recovered.

My mother was fourteen when she boarded a plane for the first time and flew to Australia. She remembers feeling torn: 'I couldn't wait to see my father and explore a new country but I felt heartbroken at the same time about having to leave my mother and siblings behind, as they relied on me so much.'

In Lebanon, Citi had relied on my mother's help to raise her children and work the land. 'I often felt like I had to carry the load of my father,' my mother says. After about four years of living in Australia, Mum had comfortably settled with her father, learned enough English to read and write, and was becoming accustomed to the Australian culture. She was considered a young woman now, which meant that she was ready for marriage. Waiting for her back in Lebanon was my father, a young man eager to start a family. A wedding was arranged.

◆ **The Family Story**

Joumana's younger sisters, Hind and Rosa, were born three years apart, but they are more like twins. They have a great relationship and are usually found bouncing off one another, telling entertaining tales. They are known for their comedy performances and off-beat stories that often make us lose ourselves in laughter. Some of my favourite stories of theirs are the ones relating to their immigration to Australia. They are both in their forties, which makes them quite youthful for aunties. I guess that's why I consider them to be more like older sisters who share with me the trials and triumphs of being women, mothers and wives stuck between two cultures. Aunty Therese is in her early forties and is the mother of four children. She hopes to pass on her culinary secrets to her children in the same way that her mother did to her.

My family members are an opinionated bunch, and I have found myself in the middle of heated battles when Mum and Aunty Rosa have been comparing their recipes for the Lebanese national dish of kibbeh. Although we have our differences, once a huge bowl of tabbouleh lands on the table, everyone helps themselves to a generous serve and eats in complete silence. It's our common bond, our connection with our elders and our ancestors.

My hope is that this book will serve as a record of the traditional Lebanese recipes perfected by these women. Although the recipes are familiar, the way my family cooks them is unique. The recipes have been passed down through generations of Taouks, but each of my aunties has her own version. And so in keeping with the Lebanese tradition of hospitality, I am delighted to share with you this banquet of treasured family recipes. *Sahtayn*!
Nouha Taouk

1
Aunty Hind
A Common Bond

The Essentials for Lebanese Cooking

'I am happiest when I am surrounded by my family. It's important for us to be gathered together doing what we love— cooking, laughing and telling stories. We learn so much from each other.' Aunty Hind

The women's kitchens are equipped with the essential ingredients and tools needed for Lebanese cooking. As in a re-interpretation of a famous play, the characters are all there, ready to perform their roles in another classic. Olive oil, cooking oils, herbs, spices, nuts, legumes and pulses are bought in bulk. Recipes that once required great effort are made easier by the use of a food processor or mincer.

Aunty Hind treasures a tradition that she started with Aunty Rosa back when they were in high school: their weekly trip to Sydney's Flemington Market and Fish Market for 'the freshest of fresh produce'. They became addicted to the variety and choice they found at these venues, so they returned to the markets when they had their own children and their vegetable gardens couldn't keep up with the demands of their families. 'When we migrated to Australia, our parents relied on the markets for buying in bulk to sustain a big family,' Aunty Hind explains.

Fridays used to begin bright and early and end in a cook-off. Back when their children were all still at school, it was easier for them to round up their families and enjoy a Friday feast at either one of their houses than cook separately. Fish was always on the menu, accompanied by a huge bowl of tabbouleh, as well as hummous, tahini sauce and plenty of pickles. Now they treat themselves to a mini cook-off lunch after their weekly excursion.

Years of trawling through the markets have enabled them to remain loyal customers to some of their favourite stores. The 'old Chinese man,' who Aunty Hind believes has been there for at least half a century, has 'the best watermelon, sweet potato, garlic and Spanish onion,' while the Lebanese guy 'never fails to deliver the finest tomatoes'. Week in, week out, the 'Italian guy and his family' expect the women of my family to come in and buy carrots, capsicums, cabbages, celery and lettuce. If they can't get to the fish markets they rely on the 'Greek guy' at Flemington. They also enjoy the opportunity to revel in each other's company. As a result they have many colourful stories to tell, many of which have entertained us during countless family cook-off sessions over the years.

One defining market experience earned Aunty Hind her title, *Mastooleh,* Arabic for 'The Statue Among The Chaos'. The buzz that circulates through the markets is usually amplified when the storeowners begin to compete against each other, raising their voices as they dramatically slash prices. On one occasion, a man selling pumpkins had begun belting out at the top of his voice, 'one dollar pumpkin, one dollar pumpkin, come and get your one dollar pumpkin before it all goes'. Aunty Rosa, who was in the middle of another purchase, turned to her sister and asked: 'Why are you standing there like a statue? Quick! Get over there—we need pumpkin'. Aunty Hind shot her a petrified look and insisted that she couldn't. Meanwhile, people were frantically grabbing boxes of pumpkins and heading off with them. Confused but eager to grab a bargain, Aunty Rosa leapt in front of her sister, picked out quality pumpkins to fill a box and without looking handed the box over to her sister. After she had paid for the box she turned back and saw her sister standing there empty handed. 'Where is the box, Hind?' Rosa asked furiously. 'The woman standing next to me grabbed it and ran,' Hind replied with a shocked look on her face.

At her best when selecting produce away from pressure and chaos, Aunty Hind explains: 'What makes me panic during these specials is the fear that I will bring home something that is spoilt and not in good condition. I love top-quality fruit and vegetables, they enhance the meals and are always a pleasure to consume'. Fastidious about selecting produce that smells and looks right, she likes to take her time. A simple tap on a watermelon will indicate whether she is in for a juicy treat. There is a certain plumpness of tomatoes that she is searching for as she feels them with her fingertips. Herbs and greens need to exude a smell of freshness when she presses them against her nose. Driven by the mantra 'fresh is best', she cooks meals that are to be eaten on the same day. Dishes are never made with the intention of going back into the fridge as they 'lose their nutritional value'.

Aunty Hind lives in the southwestern suburbs of Sydney, the hub for everything Middle Eastern—so much so that in some parts you could easily forget you are still in Australia. The Lebanese butcher in the suburb of Punchbowl takes the time to greet her with 'Keef halek?' (How are you?), as if she is an old friend visiting his home. She responds with 'Ana bikhayr, shu-ukhbaarak?' (I am well, what's your news?). The pleasantries cover news of their children, their health and the weather before exchanging money for meat. Fava beans, chickpeas and lentils, along with cumin, cinnamon, black pepper and Lebanese bread, are a few of Aunty Hind's favourite items to pick up from the Lebanese grocer in nearby Bankstown. Mounds of herbs and spices fill up the centre of the shop that is set up like a Middle Eastern souk. The gregarious nature of the shop owner always manages to steal her attention and they quickly engage in conversation that is open to anybody else who walks in. 'I feel like I am back at the village in Lebanon when I visit my local shops,' she giggles. Back there, she reminisces, 'all the houses have their doors open; the days are occupied by endless chats with anyone that they see'.

Proud of her heritage and the food that she has grown up with, she has faced up to every obstacle that has stood in the way of her being able to express who she is. She remembers the foreign sound of the English language that she could not speak, read or write when they immigrated to Australia. Her fluent Arabic and French had no place at school, where she 'stuck out like an alien'. Plonked in a classroom with students her own age, she struggled to have a voice among the sounds that were so unfamiliar to her ear. In the playground, she clung to the other ethnic girls with whom she shared a common bond. At lunchtime they opened their containers packed with olives, cheeses, cold meats and dips and spread them out like a banquet to share; a far cry from the white sliced-bread sandwiches in other lunchboxes. They were a spectacle to those who were not accustomed to the 'offensive smells' and the communal way of eating that required hands picking at the food. Sometimes the smell of raw onion or even the peculiarity of an olive resulted in schoolyard rumbles. Food would go flying through the air and harsh words were exchanged. 'Our food made us stick out like a bad smell but that never made us want to change what we ate,' says a proud Aunty Hind. 'We just paid the price and did our time with whatever words were thrown at us.'

The Essentials

You would be hard pressed not to find any of these readily available at each of the women's homes.

Garden Essentials

Most of these fresh ingredients are easy to grow at home in your own garden and some even work well in pots in a sunny spot.

Beetroot (beet)	Lettuce	Purslane (pigweed)	Tomato
Chickweed	Mint	Radish	Vine leaves from the
Cucumber	Olive tree	Rocket (arugula)	grapevine
Curly endive	Onion	Silverbeet	
Garlic	Oregano	Spinach	
Lemon	Parsley	Spring onion (scallion)	

Pantry Essentials

You can buy most of these essentials at the supermarket; the more specialised ingredients are found at Lebanese grocers. Buy the spices in small quantities so they are fresh and full of flavour.

SPICE MIXES

Baharat spice mix

A mixture of spices commonly used for seasoning, made with parts of pimento, nutmeg, cumin, cinnamon, coriander, cloves and black pepper.

My family's baharat recipe

This downsized version uses equal amounts of cumin, cinnamon and finely ground Lebanese black pepper.

Kibbeh spice mix

A mixture of cinnamon, cumin, finely ground Lebanese black pepper, basil and marjoram.

Shawarama spice mix

A mixture of cloves, cinnamon, nutmeg, pimento, paprika and finely ground Lebanese black pepper.

Shish kebab spice mix

A mixture of lemon pepper, onion, garlic, black pepper, red capsicum (pepper), salt and sugar. We use this for shish kebab but also to season other meat.

OTHER PANTRY INGREDIENTS

Ahweh (Lebanese coffee)

Barley

Borlotti beans

Broad (fava) beans

Burghul (crushed wheat)— coarse and fine

Butterbeans (lima beans)

Chickpeas (garbanzos)

Chilli powder

Cinnamon stick

Date purée

Dried oregano

Dried mint

Egg noodles

Kidney beans

Kishk granules

Lentils

Mahlab—the small kernel from a variety of cherry. It is used to flavour cakes, pastries and biscuits in Middle Eastern cooking. It has a rose fragrance and a bitter almond-like taste.

Olive oil

Orange blossom water

Pine nuts

Rosewater

Semolina

Sumac

Tahini paste

Vegetable oil

White beans

Mezze Essentials

It's easy to put together a quick mezze if you keep your kitchen stocked with these ingredients.

Almonds—soaked in water and refrigerated.
Babba ghanoush
Cashews
Hummous
Laben
Labneh
Lebanese bread
Peanuts
Pickles—cucumber, green beans, labneh balls,
    olives, stuffed eggplant and turnips
Pistachios—with or without shells

Pumpkin seeds—with or without shells
Shanklish—dried labneh balls rolled in herbs
    (see page 35)
Small lupini beans—boil and then soak in water.
    Delicious with a sprinkle of salt. Peel off the skin
    and eat the inside
Sultanas
Vegetables, sliced into crudités—carrot, capsicum
    (pepper), celery, cucumber and tomato
Walnuts—can be soaked in water and refrigerated

Kitchen Utensils

You can buy the special Lebanese implements at a Lebanese grocery store.

Colander
Falafel scoop (oleb il falafel)
Food processor
Lebanese coffee pot (rakweh)—narrow pot with a
    long handle to brew Lebanese coffee in
Ma moul mould (oleb il ma moul, taabeh or
    tamreah)— used to mould walnut and date
    biscuits (see page 230)
Mortar and pestle
Sieve
Small coffee cup (demitasse)—for drinking
    Lebanese coffee
Zucchini scoop (manerah)—used to scrape out the
    pulp from zucchini (courgettes)

Bayd ma'a batata
Egg and potato mash
serves 4

3 small potatoes
4 eggs
2 tablespoons olive oil
⅛ teaspoon ground cinnamon
⅛ teaspoon chilli powder

Peel, wash and cut the potatoes into cubes.

Boil the eggs and the potatoes separately. The eggs have to be hard boiled and the potatoes have to be tender enough to mash. Remove from the heat once they are both done, then drain off the water.

Allow both the potatoes and eggs to cool a little.

Peel and roughly chop the eggs and place them in a bowl with the potatoes. Partially mash the eggs with the potatoes, oil, cinnamon, chilli and a pinch of salt—you should still be able to see pieces of egg and potato.

Note: This is great on toast topped with sliced tomato, olives and rocket (arugula).

Bayd maqlii
Fried eggs
serves 4

olive oil, for coating the pan
4 eggs
⅛ teaspoon dried oregano
⅛ teaspoon salt
⅛ teaspoon chilli powder

Coat a large cast-iron or non-stick frying pan with oil, crack in the eggs and sprinkle oregano, salt and chilli on top. Cover the pan with a lid and cook until the egg yolk begins to just set.

Oojeh
Egg, onion and parsley pancakes
serves 4–6

5 eggs

2 tablespoons self-raising (self-rising) flour

3 onions, finely chopped

1 large handful flat-leaf (Italian) parsley, finely chopped

1 tablespoon mint, finely chopped

¼ teaspoon salt

¼ teaspoon ground cinnamon

¼ teaspoon chilli powder

¼ teaspoon finely ground Lebanese black pepper

olive oil, for coating the pan

Whisk the eggs in a bowl until fluffy. Add the flour, then the rest of the ingredients and stir.

Coat a 15 cm (6 inch) non-stick frying pan with oil and put over medium heat. Pour ½ cup of the mixture into the pan. Once the bottom is golden brown, carefully turn the pancake over to cook the other side. Remove from the pan and keep warm. Repeat with the remaining mixture.

Bayd ma'a lahm
Scrambled eggs with meat
serves 4–6

250 g (9 oz) diced lamb

¼ teaspoon my family's baharat spice mix (see page 22)

¼ teaspoon salt

⅛ teaspoon chilli powder

4 eggs

In a non-stick frying pan, combine the meat and spices. Cook, stirring, over high heat until the meat begins to brown. Reduce the heat to medium, add the eggs and stir gently to scramble the eggs. Once the eggs are fluffy and cooked, remove from the heat and serve.

Oojet kusa
Zucchini omelettes

serves 4–6

500 g (1 lb 2 oz) Lebanese (pale green)
   zucchini (courgettes)
3 eggs
75 g (2½ oz/½ cup) self-raising
   (self-rising) flour
½ small bunch flat-leaf (Italian)
   parsley, chopped
½ small bunch mint, chopped
1 onion, chopped
1 teaspoon mixed spice
1½ teaspoons salt
vegetable oil, for coating the pan

Scrape out the pulp from the inside of the zucchini. Discard the zucchini shells or reserve for another use. Place the pulp in a food processor and process until it is no longer lumpy. Transfer the zucchini to a large bowl with the rest of the ingredients and mix with a wooden spoon.

Coat a large non-stick frying pan with oil and place over medium heat. Cooking a few omelettes at a time, pour ¼ cup of the zucchini mixture into the pan for each omelette. Flatten out to about 10 cm (4 inches) in diameter. The omelettes are not supposed to look perfect in shape. Once the bottom is golden brown, turn the omelette over to cook the other side. Remove from the pan and repeat with the remaining batter.

Lay the omelettes flat on a wide dish to cool, then stack them on top of each other. Serve at room temperature or, if you prefer them hot, keep them warm in a low oven until ready to serve.

Note: This is a great recipe to make to use up the leftover zucchini pulp from stuffed zucchini (see pages 194, 198 and 211).

These omelettes taste great served with some tomato salsa (see page 49).

Laben

Home-made yoghurt

makes 4 litres (140 fl oz)

This is an example of basic fermentation, turning milk into yoghurt. Laben forms the basis of several recipes in this book and this quantity makes enough for several recipes. Laben is delicious served with a salad of cucumber, mint and garlic or spread on Lebanese bread and served with rice. If you are making laben for this purpose, make half the amount. You will need a stainless steel pan.

4 litres (140 fl oz/16 cups) full-cream (whole) milk
125 ml (4 fl oz/½ cup) traditional plain Greek-style yoghurt

Heat the milk in a large stainless steel saucepan to the point where it begins to froth and rise. Remove the pan from the heat and allow to cool to 47–50°C (117–122°F). My family use their fingers to check for the right temperature. They place their finger into the milk and count to 10 or 13. By then the heat should be unbearable. You can either place the pan in cold water for a speedy temperature drop or just set it aside to cool naturally.

Dissolve the yoghurt in a small bowl with some of the warm milk. Add the dissolved yoghurt to the rest of the warm milk and stir.

Put the pan in an undisturbed place that is warm and away from any breeze. Cover the pan with its lid, then wrap the entire pan with layers of woollen blankets or any warm covers, ideally no less than five layers. Leave it wrapped for at least 6 hours or overnight.

Unwrap the blankets and remove the lid. Shake the pan slightly. The laben should have a jelly-like consistency. Cover the pan with the lid and store the laben in the coldest part of the fridge. It has to stay there for 2 days before you can break the laben and eat it. The laben can be sweetened with sugar.

Labneh
Creamy home-made yoghurt
serves 6-8

This is home-made yoghurt (laben) that is made creamier by extracting the fluid from it. Use the same procedure as for making laben (see opposite page). Labneh is lovely scooped up with a piece of Lebanese bread or a cracker as part of a banquet.

1 tablespoon salt
2 litres (70 fl oz/8 cups) laben that has
   been in the fridge for 2 days (see
   opposite page)
chilli powder, to serve
olive oil, to serve

Mix the salt with the laben. Pour the laben into a cotton sack (similar to a pillow case) or piece of muslin (cheesecloth) and drain out the fluid by either hanging it outside (if the weather is moderate, hang in the shade away from direct sunlight) or in a strainer suspended over a bowl in the fridge. Drain in the sack overnight.

The next day open the sack and pour and scrape out the thick creamy labneh from inside the sack into a bowl. Stir together the different parts of the labneh so the different textures merge together—you should end up with a texture similar to thick cream. Discard everything on the outside of the sack.

You can eat the labneh straight away or store it in the fridge. It will last for up to 2 weeks. To serve, sprinkle it with some chilli powder and drizzle some olive oil on top.

Shanklish

Dried labneh cheese balls

makes 5

This recipe starts by using the same procedure as making labneh from laben but, if you prefer, you can skip that step and buy the labneh ready-made from most Lebanese grocery stores. If you buy ready-made labneh, skip ahead to adding the chilli powder. Shanklish balls are usually served as part of a banquet.

2 litres (70 fl oz/8 cups) laben that
   has been in the fridge for 2 days
   (see page 30)
2–3 tablespoons salt
½–1 teaspoon mild chilli powder
100 g (3½ oz) dried oregano or thyme

Put the laben and salt in a stainless steel saucepan and bring to the boil. Boil for 2 minutes, then turn the heat off and straight away tip the mixture into a cotton sack (similar to a pillow case) or piece of muslin (cheesecloth) and drain out the fluid by either hanging it outside (if the weather is moderate, hang it in the shade away from direct sunlight) or in a strainer suspended over a bowl in the fridge. Drain in the sack for 2–3 days, discarding any excess liquid every day. You'll know it's ready when the mixture is dry and hard enough to roll.

On a flat tray, lay a cotton sheet or kitchen towel. The sheet will absorb any moisture from the balls.

Remove the mixture from the sack and place in a bowl.

If you are using ready-made labneh, put it in a bowl.

Add the chilli powder to taste to the home-made or ready-made labneh and mix with your hands. Roll the mixture with your hands into rounds the size of a tennis ball, then roll in the oregano or thyme. Place on the tray and cover with a cotton sheet or kitchen towel. Set aside for 3 days in a cool, dry spot, away from direct sunlight, or in the fridge.

You can eat the shanklish straight away or store in a container in the fridge for up to 2 weeks. The longer you store them in the fridge the more pungent the flavour. These are delicious crumbled, drizzled with olive oil, and served with finely diced onion wrapped in Lebanese bread.

Rooz bi haleeb
Breakfast rice pudding

serves 4

This lovely rice and milk dish is served for breakfast and is great enjoyed hot or cold.

1 litre (35 fl oz/4 cups) milk
165 g (5¾ oz/¾ cup) medium-grain rice
1 teaspoon salt

Put the milk and 125 ml (4 fl oz/½ cup) of water in a saucepan over high heat and bring to the boil. Add the rice and salt, then stir while bringing back to the boil. Once the mixture has returned to the boil, reduce the heat and simmer for 15 minutes or until the rice is cooked and tender.

Note: If you are serving the rice cold, cool it to room temperature, then refrigerate.

Rooz il falfal
Boiled rice with egg noodles

serves 6

This is a general rice recipe that accompanies many of the casserole dishes. Another version of this dish is to cook the rice and noodles, then allow it to cool a little, then mix it with 2–3 tablespoons of laben (see page 30).

40 g (1½ oz) butter
2 balls (130 g/4½ oz total) dried fine egg noodles (see Note)
370 g (13 oz/2 cups) medium-grain rice, washed very well (see Note)
½ teaspoon salt

Melt the butter in a saucepan over low heat. Break the noodles into small pieces with your hands and add to the pan. Stir occasionally until golden brown. Mix in the rice and salt. Add 1.125 litres (39 fl oz/4½ cups) of water and bring to the boil. Cover with a lid once boiled, then reduce the heat and simmer for 15 minutes or until the rice is cooked.

Note: The noodles are available from a Lebanese grocer. We have used medium-grain rice, but you can make this with long-grain rice, if you prefer.

Hummous

makes 4 cups

Hummous is treated like a condiment in our family. I remember as a child Mum would always make sure that there was a fresh batch of hummous made before we got to the end of the previous batch. Both hummous and babba ghanoush go well with almost any Lebanese dish. You can dip bread, or fresh or pickled vegetables into it.

300 g (10½ oz/1½ cups) dried
   chickpeas (garbanzos)
½ teaspoon bicarbonate of soda
   (baking soda)
1 garlic clove, crushed
1½ teaspoons salt
135 g (4¾ oz/½ cup) tahini
80–100 ml (2½–3½ fl oz) lemon juice
chilli powder, paprika or cayenne
   pepper, to serve
olive oil, to serve
finely chopped flat-leaf (Italian)
   parsley, to serve

Soak the chickpeas in water overnight.

Add the bicarbonate of soda to the soaking liquid and soak for an extra 30 minutes. Rinse the chickpeas well, then strain and pour into a saucepan. Add about three times the amount of water to the chickpeas (the chickpeas should be drowning in water). Boil the chickpeas for about 40 minutes until they are super soft—they should almost melt when pressed between your fingers. (If your chickpeas are old, they will need more cooking time.)

Remove the pan from the heat and allow the chickpeas to cool in the cooking liquid. (Do not rinse them in cold water.) Once they have cooled, collect 250 ml (9 fl oz/1 cup) of the cooking liquid and set aside. Drain the chickpeas in a strainer.

Place the chickpeas in a food processor, add the garlic and 1 teaspoon of the salt and process until a crumbled paste begins to form. Add the tahini and process—the paste should be getting softer now. Drizzle in 4 tablespoons of the lemon juice and continue to process, then drizzle in some of the reserved cooking liquid until you get a creamy purée. Season to taste, adding the rest of the salt and lemon juice if you like.

Hummous is usually served as part of a banquet. It is usually spread over a round or oval platter. A spoon is used to create a circular or oval ridge in the middle. Chilli powder, paprika or cayenne pepper is sprinkled along the ridge followed by a swirl of olive oil. Finely chopped parsley is also sprinkled over the top as a garnish.

Note: The hummous will keep for about a week in the fridge.

Babba ghanoush

makes 2 cups

'Barbecued eggplant is great for a smoky flavour.' Aunty Hind

2 medium eggplants (aubergines)
90 g (3¼ oz/⅓ cup) tahini
juice of 1–2 lemons
2 garlic cloves
½–1 teaspoon salt
olive oil, to serve
finely chopped flat-leaf (Italian)
   parsley, to serve
finely diced tomato, to serve

Pierce holes into the skin of the eggplants with a fork or skewer. Leave the stem on the eggplants—you will need it as a handle later.

There are three methods of cooking the eggplants, but whichever method you use, cook them until you are sure that they are completely soft. To test if the eggplants are cooked, poke them with your tongs—they should sink right through into the flesh.

<u>**Barbecue:**</u> Place the eggplants on the barbecue and keep turning them over until they soften.

<u>**Stove:**</u> Place the eggplants on top of the gas flame or hotplate and use the stem or tongs to turn them over.

Oven: Bake in a preheated 200–230°C (400–450°F) oven for up to 20 minutes.

Once the eggplants are cooked, place them in cold water and allow to cool enough to touch, then peel off the skins with a small, sharp knife; remove the stems. Transfer the pulp to a strainer and leave to drain for 10–15 minutes. Place the pulp into a bowl and mash with a masher or a fork until most off the bigger lumps are gone.

Mix in the tahini and the juice of 1 lemon. Crush the garlic with a little salt using a mortar and pestle until very soft and creamy. Add the crushed garlic and ½ teaspoon salt to the eggplant and mix together. Season to taste, adding more salt or lemon juice as desired.

Scoop the babba ghanoush onto a serving plate. Garnish with a drizzle of olive oil, finely chopped parsley and finely diced tomato.

Cooking *with* Intuition

Before we get too far into the book, we need to talk about intuition versus measurements. When the editor of this book sent me a Recipe Measuring Style Guide, I felt slightly panicked. The same panic I still feel when I am in my kitchen and have to call Mum to help me figure out why my falafel is sloppy and fragmented when I try to fry it. There is never a question about whether I have followed the correct measurements or not, because there aren't any to begin with. Instead Mum tells me the answer over the phone: 'Flour, Nouha, you need flour'. (Flour is an ingredient that is only included in desperate times like these.)

In our family kitchens, measuring utensils are traded in for intuition. Cooking comes from the heart and food is always made with the intention of sharing with and pleasing others. You learn to cook through tasting, feeling and connecting with the food. Fulfilling the appetite and providing satisfaction is the culturally embedded way with which we communicate, connect and show our love.

So, figuring out the measurements for most of these recipes was a frustrating task for me. When I caught up with the women featured in this book to document the recipes, I was armed with measuring spoons, measuring cups and a scale. I can't begin to tell you how many times I had to wave those instruments around as a reminder to 'think measurements!'.

Each woman has her sense of style, her own personal attributes. Although I have managed to provide you with 'our measurements', I hope that when you learn to cook these recipes and

become confident with the ingredients and methods, you will also liberate yourself from the measuring tools. Most of the recipes are simple, and while the ingredients and the techniques may seem repetitive, the outcome is always different. Garlic, onion and tomato make regular appearances to produce tasty variants of dishes such as Okra and lamb casserole (see page 72) and Green bean and lamb casserole (see page 84). For some recipes, a decision to intentionally reduce the amount of garlic, onion and chilli had to be made. It became apparent that one whole bulb of garlic for something like Silverbeet and lentil soup (see page 92) may be too overwhelming for those not accustomed to it. So instead six cloves are recommended to begin with, which you can add to as you become accustomed to the pungent taste of the garlic.

When you set out to cook some of these recipes it's not just the ingredients and the method that are essential for success. You also need to remember to switch on your intuition, embrace your senses and set the right ambience. In our family kitchens, bad moods are not welcome. I was never allowed to assist Mum with her cooking if I was in a bad mood. She believes that it compromises the end result. 'If you cook with love, then you produce love,' she always preached to me.

Our mantra: Cook with love using fresh produce, season to taste and always eat to share.

Taratoor/Toum

Garlic sauce

makes 310 ml (10¾ fl oz)

Use this as a sauce for barbecued meats or as a sauce for a falafel.

125 ml (4 fl oz/½ cup) olive oil
125 ml (4 fl oz/½ cup) vegetable oil
12 garlic cloves
¼ teaspoon salt, or to taste
juice of 1 lemon

Combine the two oils in a jug.

Put the garlic and salt in a narrow jug. Purée the garlic and salt with a stick blender while slowing drizzling in a little of the oil mixture. Stop occasionally to scrape the mixture from the sides of the jug. As you do this, the mixture should gradually become creamier. Keep going, very gradually adding the oil, until all of the oil is used up. If the mixture begins to split when adding the oil, then drizzle in some of the lemon juice to thicken. Otherwise, once the oil is completed, drizzle in about 2 tablespoons of lemon juice and blend. Taste and add more lemon or salt as desired.

Note: You could also make this sauce in a mortar and pestle. The addition of a cooked and peeled potato to this sauce will soften the garlic flavour and it will also fix the sauce if you have added the oil too quickly.

Tahini ma'a haamid wa toum

Tahini with lemon and garlic

makes 310 ml (10¾ fl oz)

3 garlic cloves
¼ teaspoon salt
205 g (7¼ oz/¾ cup) tahini
juice of 2 lemons

Crush the garlic with a little of the salt using a mortar and pestle until the garlic is soft and silky.

Blend the garlic, tahini, lemon juice, remaining salt and a little water in a food processor. The sauce should be slightly runny—add a little more water as necessary. Season to taste.

Tahini salsa

Tahini sauce with tomato and parsley

makes 310 ml (10¾ fl oz)

2 garlic cloves
½ teaspoon salt
135 g (4¾ oz/½ cup) tahini
juice of 2 lemons
1 tomato, finely chopped
1 tablespoon finely chopped flat-leaf
   (Italian) parsley

Crush the garlic with the salt using a mortar and pestle until the garlic is soft and silky.

Pour the tahini into a bowl, add the garlic and stir (use the pestle to mix). Add the lemon juice and a little, water little by little, and keep stirring until it is a creamy consistency.

Mix in the tomato and parsley. Season to taste.

Jibneh layyin
Lebanese loose cheese

makes 10

You will need a 2 litre (70 fl oz/8 cup) sterilised glass jar for this recipe. It is ideal with vegetables.

4 litres (140 fl oz/16 cups) full-cream
   (whole) milk
¼ teaspoon junket powder or finely
   crushed junket tablet
salt

In a large saucepan, warm the milk over medium heat to 43°C (109°F). Remove the pan from the heat and stir the milk well for about 1 minute. Add the junket and stir again, preferably using your hands, making sure the junket has dissolved. Place the lid on the pan and cover with a woollen blanket to insulate for 1 hour.

Uncover the pan and, using your hand again, stir through. Make sure as you are stirring that your fingers are separated, allowing the milk mixture to swim through. Stir for about 30 seconds. Fragmented sponge-like pieces will start to form among the liquid. Pull the sponge-like cheese into a mound, then gently push down onto it with a medium or large sieve and scoop out the liquid within the strainer with a ladle or cup. Keep doing this until most of the liquid is emptied and all you have is the cheese.

With your hand, scoop out enough cheese to sit in your palm to create a thick patty. Gently squeeze out any remaining liquid as you mould a thick cheese patty that is about 3 cm (1¼ inches) thick and 8–10 cm (3¼–4 inches) in diameter. Place the patty in a large strainer that has been lined with cotton or muslin (cheesecloth) and is sitting over a bowl. Continue to shape the patties. Keep turning the finished patties over every 5 minutes so they do not loose their shape. Stand until the excess liquid has drained off; this takes up to 1 hour.

Once all the water has drained off, lay on a cold tray. You can add salt to taste to the cheese right away or refrigerate for 2 days without being salted.

If you want to store the cheese for longer, sprinkle it with ½ teaspoon salt. Boil 1 litre (35 fl oz/4 cups) of water with 1 tablespoon sea salt for 30 minutes and cool overnight. Put the cheese in a 2 litre (70 fl oz/8 cup) sterilised glass jar, then cover with the brine. Keep in the fridge for up to 1 week.

Salsat banadoora
Tomato salsa
makes 1.5 litres (52 fl oz)

This salsa is an ideal condiment for barbecues, boiled potatoes and to use as a sauce for cooking stews and casseroles. It can easily be halved, if you want to make less.

2 kg (4 lb 8 oz) soft cooking tomatoes, core removed and cut into quarters, reserving any juices

16 garlic cloves

1½ tablespoons salt

2 granny smith apples, peeled, cored and diced

3 brown onions, chopped

3 small red chillies, seeded and chopped

In a large saucepan over medium heat, cook the tomatoes in their own juices for about 10 minutes, stirring occasionally, until they soften. Pour the tomatoes and their juices into a sieve over a bowl. Press the tomato against the sieve or use a mouli to release as much juice as possible from the tomato into the bowl. Discard the pulp.

Return the tomato juice to the pan with the rest of the ingredients and bring to the boil over high heat, stirring occasionally. Reduce the heat and keep stirring for up to 1 hour or until the apple and garlic are soft. Lightly mash to break up some of the chunks. Season to taste.

Note: Store the salsa in sterilised glass jars and refrigerate once opened.

Dummus fool
Lightly crushed broad beans with olive oil

serves 6

This dip is called dummus fool when made with broad beans and dummus hummous when made with chickpeas. Here it has been made with half of each. Serve it for breakfast with eggs or as part of a banquet.

150 g (5½ oz/1 cup) dried broad (fava) beans or 220 g (7¾ oz/1 cup) dried chickpeas (garbanzos) or ½ cup of each
1 garlic clove
juice of 1 lemon
1 small handful flat-leaf (Italian) parsley, finely chopped
½ teaspoon salt
1 tablespoon extra virgin olive oil

Soak the broad beans or chickpeas in water overnight. Rinse and drain.

Boil the broad beans or chickpeas or both in separate pans of water until tender—broad beans will need about 1 hour and chickpeas about 30–40 minutes. Strain and cool.

Crush the garlic with a sprinkle of the salt using a large mortar and pestle.

Add the beans or chickpeas and gently crush with a pestle or a masher. The beans will form a tiny crack but will hold their form—the crack will help them absorb flavour. Add the rest of the ingredients and toss together.

Khobz maqli
Fried bread

serves 6

500 ml (17 fl oz/2 cups) vegetable oil
6 pieces Lebanese bread, cut into triangles to fit the frying pan

Heat the oil in a large frying pan until hot. Fry the bread, in batches, turning once, for up to 30 seconds or until golden and crisp, then drain on kitchen paper.

Salatat il hindbeh

Endive salad

serves 4

1 bunch curly endive
4 tomatoes, chopped
1 garlic clove
¼ teaspoon salt, or to taste
1 tablespoon extra virgin olive oil
juice of 1 lemon

Wash the endive and discard the bottom stems. Cut the bunch of leaves into three to four chunks. Put in a salad bowl with the diced tomato.

Crush the garlic with a sprinkle of salt using a mortar and pestle. Add the oil and lemon juice. Season to taste. Add to the salad bowl and toss together.

Sleeh maslooh

Blanched endive salad

serves 4

1 bunch curly endive
2 garlic cloves
¼ teaspoon salt, or to taste
1 tablespoon extra virgin olive oil
juice of 1 lemon

Wash the endive and discard the bottom stems. Cut the bunch of leaves into three to four chunks.

Place the endive to a saucepan of boiling salted water and cook for up to 30 minutes or until very tender. The endive will change colour from light green to dark green. Transfer to a colander and allow to cool.

Once cooled, grab a bunch of leaves and roll into a ball to fit into your hands. Squeeze as much excess liquid while retaining the shape of the ball. Put the leaves in a bowl.

Crush the garlic with a sprinkle of salt using a mortar and pestle. Add the oil and lemon juice. Season to taste. Add to the bowl and toss together.

Khiyaar bi laben
Yoghurt and cucumber salad

serves 4–6

This is fantastic to eat on its own or as a side during summer, especially chilled.

6 Lebanese (short) cucumbers
2 garlic cloves
¼ teaspoon salt
1 teaspoon dried mint, plus extra,
   to serve
500 ml (17 fl oz/2 cups) plain yoghurt
   or laben (see page 30)

Wash the cucumbers and trim the both ends. Peel, leaving some strips of the skin. Slice them lengthways down the middle and chop into pieces.

Crush the garlic with a sprinkle of salt and the mint using a mortar and pestle. Transfer the garlic and mint paste to a bowl and add the yoghurt. Stir to combine and season to taste. Add the cucumber and mix well. Transfer to a serving bowl and sprinkle with extra dried mint.

Note: Cold pasta, such as spaghetti, can be added to this salad.

Salatat malfoof
Green cabbage salad

serves 6

2 garlic cloves
⅛ teaspoon salt
½ head small green cabbage, shredded
juice of 2 lemons
1 tablespoon extra virgin olive oil
2 tomatoes, chopped

Crush the garlic cloves with a sprinkle of salt using a mortar and pestle.

Combine all of the ingredients in a salad bowl and toss. Season to taste.

Note: Green cabbage salad goes well with Lentils and rice (see page 164).

Tabbouleh

serves 6

✕—✕—✕

Most of my family prefer to make this fresh green salad without the burghul. Try it with burghul and without to decide which version you prefer.

45 g (1¾ oz/¼ cup) fine crushed wheat
  (burghul), optional

3 bunches flat-leaf (Italian) parsley

1 small handful mint

5 vine-ripened tomatoes

1 teaspoon salt, or to taste

½ teaspoon sumac

⅛ teaspoon chilli powder

¼ teaspoon finely ground Lebanese
  black pepper

1 red onion, finely chopped

125 ml (4 fl oz/½ cup) lemon juice

2 tablespoons extra virgin olive oil

If you are using burghul, wash it and drain well.

Wash the bunches of parsley in the sink, then soak in water with a sprinkle of salt. Drain, then wash thoroughly until there is no more dirt, shaking between washes. The bunches can be hung to dry or laid on a cotton sheet or kitchen towel.

Traditionally my family untie the bunches, then spread the sprigs of parsley over a cotton sheet or kitchen towel to dry. Neat bunches are then made by adding one sprig at a time to make an even bunch where the flat leaves sit evenly. Uneven offshoots are broken off and realigned in one hand to form an even bouquet. The leaves are levelled and the stems are cut off. This arduous process was the only downside to making my favourite salad. I now cheat and keep the bunches as I bought them (tied up). I cut off the stems, then continue in the way I was taught.

Finely chop the parsley leaves and transfer to a bowl. Finely chop the mint and add to the parsley. If you are using crushed wheat (burgul), squeeze out any liquid from it, then add it to the bowl with the herbs.

Dice the tomatoes and place in a sieve over a bowl to drain and prevent sogginess. Some of the juice from the tomato can be used in the tabbouleh. Add the tomato and some of the juice to the herbs.

Rub the salt, sumac, chilli powder and black pepper into the chopped onion and add to the herbs. Add the lemon juice and oil and toss, either using your hands or salad spoons. Taste and add more seasoning, oil or lemon to suit your palate.

Note: You should end up with about 160 g (5¾ oz/3 large handfuls) of parsley once chopped.

Fattoush

serves 6

'This is our quick throw together salad of vegetables picked from our gardens. The pigweed is the predominant flavour—the other ingredients shouldn't dominate it but enhance it.' Aunty Therese

1 large handful pigweed (purslane) (see Note)

2 small garlic cloves

½–1 teaspoon salt

4 tablespoons extra virgin olive oil, plus extra, for drizzling

3 vine-ripened tomatoes, roughly chopped

2 Lebanese (short) cucumbers, halved and sliced

2 radishes and their leaves, washed and sliced

½ red onion, thinly sliced

1 small handful flat-leaf (Italian) parsley

1 small handful mint, roughly chopped

juice of ½ lemon

½ teaspoon sumac

Lebanese bread, split in half, to serve

Wash the pigweed either in the sink or in a bowl. The leaves are delicate, so make sure to handle with care. Drain and pick the leaves off and set aside.

Crush the garlic with a sprinkle of salt using a mortar and pestle. Put the garlic, oil and ½ teaspoon of salt in a salad bowl and stir together until the salt dissolves. Add the vegetables, herbs, lemon juice and sumac and toss together. Taste the salad and add the rest of the salt if desired.

Bake or grill (broil) the Lebanese bread until crispy. The crispy bread is usually served on a side plate. Pieces of the bread are broken and added to individual serves. Alternatively, you can add the bread pieces to the salad bowl and drizzle with oil. This dish is ideally eaten with your hands.

Note: Buy pigweed from your greengrocer—Lebanese, Asian or Italian grocers are the most likely to stock it. Alternatively, it's easy to grow in your garden. If it is out of season, you can substitute watercress, as we have done here.

Salatat Lubnaniyeh

Lebanese salad

serves 4

1 garlic clove, crushed

¼ teaspoon salt

1 tablespoon extra virgin olive oil

juice of 1 lemon

4 Lebanese (short) cucumbers, chopped

2 tomatoes, chopped

1 handful flat-leaf (Italian) parsley,
   chopped

1 small handful mint, chopped

1 red onion, thinly sliced

Crush the garlic with a sprinkle of salt using a mortar and pestle. Add the oil, lemon juice and remaining salt and stir together. Season to taste.

Combine the remaining ingredients in a salad bowl, toss with the dressing and serve.

Salatat baleh

Pigweed salad

serves 4

1 large handful pigweed (purslane)
   (see Note)

2 garlic cloves

¼ teaspoon salt

1 tablespoon extra virgin olive oil

juice of 1 lemon

2 Lebanese (short) cucumbers, diced

2 tomatoes, diced

Wash the pigweed either in the sink or in a bowl. The leaves are delicate, so make sure to handle with care. Drain and pick the leaves off and put in a salad bowl.

Crush the garlic with a sprinkle of salt using a mortar and pestle. Add the oil, lemon juice and remaining salt and stir together. Season to taste, then add to the bowl. Add the rest of the ingredients, toss well and serve.

Note: Buy pigweed from your greengrocer—Lebanese, Asian or Italian grocers are the most likely to stock it. Alternatively, it's easy to grow in your garden. If it is out of season, you can substitute watercress.

Salatat shanklish
Shanklish salad

serves 4

2 witlofs (chicory/Belgian endive),
  leaves separated

1 baby cos lettuce, leaves separated

1 bunch rocket (arugula), larger leaves
  are best, trimmed

1 red onion, thinly sliced

4 radishes, washed, halved and sliced

2 Lebanese (short) cucumbers, diced

juice of 1 lemon

1 tablespoon extra virgin olive oil

¼ teaspoon salt

1 shanklish ball (see page 35)

Place the salad leaves and vegetables in a salad bowl. Mix the lemon juice, oil and salt together. Add to the bowl and toss everything together. Crumble the shanklish over the top.

Salatat shanklish basiita
Simple shanklish salad

serves 4

If your shanklish balls are very small, you can use two here. Shanklish salads are served as part of a banquet.

1 tomato, finely diced

1 small red onion, finely chopped

1 handful flat-leaf (Italian) parsley,
  chopped

1 shanklish ball (see page 35)

1 tablespoon extra virgin olive oil

¼ teaspoon salt

Combine the vegetables and parsley in a salad bowl. Crumble the shanklish into the bowl. Add the oil, sprinkle in the salt and toss together.

Salatat dimaagh il ghanem
Sheep's brain salad

serves 8–12

This salad is somewhat of an acquired taste, but well worth trying. It can be served as a starter or as part of a banquet, as here, or as a main meal and eaten with bread.

6 sheep's brains
1 teaspoon salt
1 cinnamon stick
2 tablespoons chopped flat-leaf (Italian) parsley
2 teaspoons finely chopped mint
2 garlic cloves
½ teaspoon chilli powder, optional
juice of 1 lemon
1 tablespoon extra virgin olive oil

Wash the brains well to remove any blood. Put the brains in a saucepan and cover with water. Add the salt and cinnamon and bring to the boil. Boil for 10–15 minutes. Pour into a strainer and drain off the water. Allow the brains to cool.

Peel away any membrane, if required, and separate the lobes in the middle. Cut each lobe into two pieces. Add to a salad bowl with the herbs.

Crush the garlic with a sprinkle of salt using a mortar and pestle. Add the chilli powder (if using), lemon juice and olive oil and mix together. Add the dressing to the bowl and toss everything together.

62

Salatat banadoora wa nahnah
Tomato and dried mint salad
serves 4

3 tomatoes, finely diced
1 red onion, finely chopped
1 garlic clove
⅛ teaspoon salt, or to taste
½ teaspoon dried mint
1 tablespoon extra virgin olive oil

Combine the tomato and onion in a large bowl. Crush the garlic with the salt using a mortar and pestle. Add the mint and the oil to the garlic and stir. Pour the dressing onto the tomato and onion and toss.

Note: Tomato and dried mint salad goes well with Lentils and rice (see page 164).

Za'atar
My family's za'atar spice mix
makes 1½ cups

110 g (3¾ oz/⅔ cup) sesame seeds
40 g (1½ oz/⅓ cup) dried thyme
60 g (2¼ oz/½ cup) sumac
1¼ teaspoons salt

Lightly toast the sesame seeds in a non-stick frying pan over high heat, continuously stirring, until light golden. Remove from the pan and cool to room temperature. Combine with the remaining ingredients in a bowl. Store in an airtight jar for up to 3 months.

2

Aunty Rosa
The Sacred Garden

Planting for the Appetite

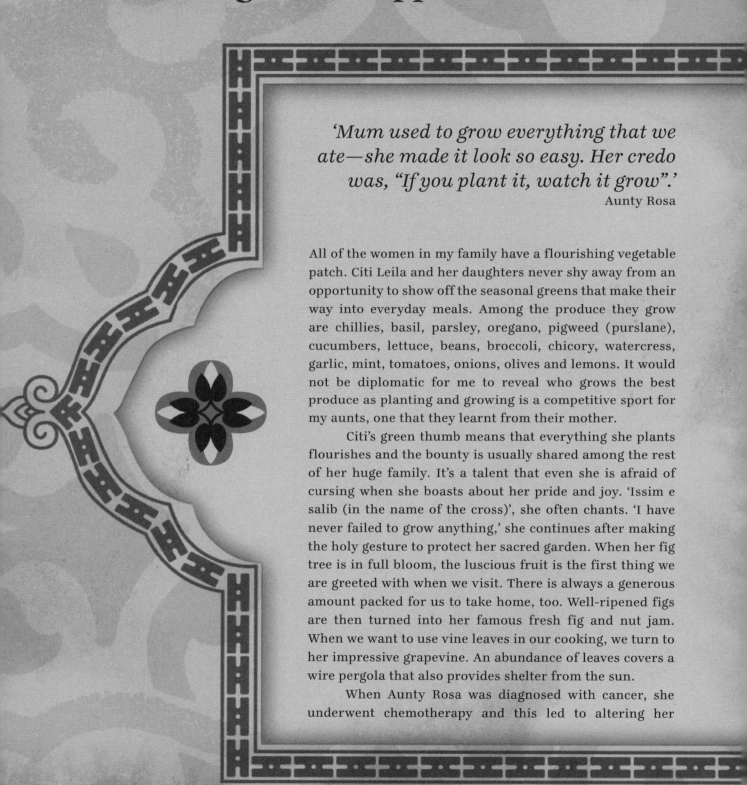

'Mum used to grow everything that we ate—she made it look so easy. Her credo was, "If you plant it, watch it grow".'
Aunty Rosa

All of the women in my family have a flourishing vegetable patch. Citi Leila and her daughters never shy away from an opportunity to show off the seasonal greens that make their way into everyday meals. Among the produce they grow are chillies, basil, parsley, oregano, pigweed (purslane), cucumbers, lettuce, beans, broccoli, chicory, watercress, garlic, mint, tomatoes, onions, olives and lemons. It would not be diplomatic for me to reveal who grows the best produce as planting and growing is a competitive sport for my aunts, one that they learnt from their mother.

Citi's green thumb means that everything she plants flourishes and the bounty is usually shared among the rest of her huge family. It's a talent that even she is afraid of cursing when she boasts about her pride and joy. 'Issim e salib (in the name of the cross)', she often chants. 'I have never failed to grow anything,' she continues after making the holy gesture to protect her sacred garden. When her fig tree is in full bloom, the luscious fruit is the first thing we are greeted with when we visit. There is always a generous amount packed for us to take home, too. Well-ripened figs are then turned into her famous fresh fig and nut jam. When we want to use vine leaves in our cooking, we turn to her impressive grapevine. An abundance of leaves covers a wire pergola that also provides shelter from the sun.

When Aunty Rosa was diagnosed with cancer, she underwent chemotherapy and this led to altering her vegetable patch. Both she and her husband Tony began to grow more silverbeet and spinach in order to boost her iron intake. Our family has always used traditional Middle Eastern silverbeet and lentil soup for medicinal purposes. Each of the aunties made sure that there was always a batch available to their sister during her treatment. When I ask Aunty Rosa about the significance of her vegetable garden she tells me that, 'I like the thought that I have grown it, that it has come straight from the garden to the family table'. Her illness also shifted her focus to the nutritional value of food, prompting her to learn more about the health benefits of everything growing in her garden. 'We have always had a healthy diet,' she explains, 'but the emphasis now is on acknowledging the health benefits rather than the taste when adding things like mint or parsley to a dish.'

The garden is her private domain, a tiny reminder of the country life she left behind as a youth in Lebanon. Talking about it brings back fond memories that transport her back to the time when she was a child living in the village of Becharee and anticipating the coming of spring. After being trapped inside for up to three months by the winter snow, the simple joy of freedom promised by the warmer months meant that the arrival of spring and summer were treated with glee: 'We were like birds out of a cage'. She was always relieved to shed the layers of clothing and begin a countdown to the long school break that lasted right through summer. She kept her ear out for the sound of running water, which signified the thawing of a nearby waterfall that officially marked the end of winter. The melting snow revealed their playground—fruit orchards in which Aunty Rosa and the children from the village would spend their days climbing and eating from. They couldn't wait for the fruit to grow fat, ripe and juicy, but one of Aunty Rosa's favourite treats was sour, unripe apples. 'I enjoyed their flavour right through the season until they were ripe,' she recalls. Once the apples had ripened, she cut off their tops, scraped out the pulp and ate it until only the thin layer of skin was left. Then she would fill them up with blueberries or mulberries to create a breakfast treat.

Summer was the busiest time of the year. There was endless produce that needed to be cultivated and harvested to sustain them through the year. 'The entire community got together,' explains Aunty Rosa, 'making sure that the soil was enriched for the crop to produce its best.' The warmer seasons provided fresh produce that they could pick and eat. During late summer and early autumn the family would begin pickling and preserving in order to prepare for when the first snows of winter blanketed the mountains again.

Citi inherited a potato farm from her father. The family grew, picked and boxed potatoes and apples which they sold. 'We learned how to select the cream of the crop, which was then exported to a demanding overseas market,' explains a proud Aunty Rosa. A fond memory of being with her mother and siblings in the potato fields springs to her mind. 'It was heading towards the end of a laborious day,' she explains. Being out in the field all day had made them exceptionally hungry and tired, but 'suddenly, a man appeared carrying trays of our favourite desserts'. This merchant wanted to barter sweets for potatoes. As a treat, Citi bought three large trays of namoora, harrisse and footeeyeah, and handed them over to her children. She then assisted the man in selecting his potatoes. By the time she got back to her children, they were lying on their backs with aching bellies, three empty trays beside them.

'It took a while before I could have any of those sweets again,' Aunty Rosa laughs.

This self-sufficient lifestyle brought my family close to the land and gave them an understanding of the seasons. They were attuned to the land, explains Aunty Rosa. 'Spring began with pears, then the apples, followed by the cherries, apricots, peaches and towards the end we expected plums,' she explains. Milk, cheeses, laben and labneh were all produced from the one goat—'our pet with benefits,' as she jokingly refers to it. The olive groves offered much more than just olives. This was where my family made their olive oil and olive butter, along with olive oil soaps.

'I found life in Australia incredibly boring when we first moved here,' Aunty Rosa admits. It was a culture shock for a young girl who loved climbing trees and picking fruit. She missed the early morning alarm clock of the roosters. 'We took turns to set the chickens free and then return them back to their pens before the sun came down and the foxes came out'. Otherwise, she says, 'that would have been the end of eggs and chicken on the menu'.

Sydney's neat rows of brick houses were quite different to the homes that were perched precariously on the side of the mountain back in Lebanon. Aunty Rosa couldn't understand why Australian houses had fences in the backyard or why they needed to be separated from their neighbours. 'I felt incredibly claustrophobic and my only saving grace was the mulberry tree at the far end of our backyard, she remembers. 'I spent most of my time after school there, eating and climbing on it. It was the closest thing to home.' Soon enough an apricot tree was planted and slowly as her parents became accustomed to this new land, they began to grow things just as they had back home.

Bemeh ma'a lahem
Okra and lamb casserole

serves 6

1 kg (2 lb 4 oz) okra

4 tablespoons olive oil

60 g (2¼ oz) butter

3 onions, cut into chunky pieces

500 g (1 lb 2 oz) lamb leg, cut into 2.5 cm (1 inch) dice

2 tablespoons tomato paste (concentrated purée)

4 soft cooking tomatoes, blanched, peeled and diced

6 garlic cloves, left whole

1 tablespoon chopped coriander (cilantro)

1 teaspoon salt

1½ teaspoons my family's baharat spice mix (see page 22)

⅛ teaspoon chilli powder, optional

juice of 1 lemon

Wash the okra thoroughly, then dry it completely by wrapping in a kitchen towel and gently pressing. Gently remove the stems by scraping around the edge with a knife. Make sure not to cut too much off, otherwise it will ooze a gel-like liquid and become difficult to cook with.

Working in batches, heat the oil in a large frying pan over medium heat. Lay the okra neatly in the pan, lining them up side by side to fill the base. Cook the okra on each side until slightly softened. Remove from the pan and drain on either a flat strainer or on kitchen paper. Repeat with the remaining okra, adding more oil, if necessary.

Heat the butter in a large saucepan over medium–low heat and cook the onion until soft and translucent. Add the lamb and cook, stirring occasionally, until lightly browned. Add 375 ml (13 fl oz/1½ cups) of water and bring to the boil over high heat. Once the liquid boils, cover the pan and reduce the heat to a simmer for 30 minutes, or until the meat is tender.

Dilute the tomato paste in 3 tablespoons of water and add to the pan along with the tomato, garlic, coriander, salt baharat and chilli powder, if using. Gently stir in the okra to mix through. Place the lid back on the pan and simmer for 10 minutes. Serve drizzled with lemon juice. This is ideal served with Boiled rice with egg noodles (see page 36).

Loubyeah otah
Vegetarian green bean casserole
serves 4–6

It is important to make sure that the beans are cooked before you add the tomatoes. The acidity of tomatoes prevents the beans from cooking further.

1 kg (2 lb 4 oz) green beans
6 garlic cloves
170 ml (5½ fl oz/⅔ cup) olive oil
2 brown onions, chopped
1 teaspoon salt
1 long red or green chilli, seeded and
   chopped, optional (see Note)
3 soft cooking tomatoes, blanched,
   peeled and diced
½ teaspoon ground cumin
½ teaspoon finely ground Lebanese
   black pepper, optional (see Note)

Trim the beans then, depending on their size, break them into two or three pieces. Wash and drain them.

Slice 3 of the garlic cloves into three pieces and keep the other cloves uncut.

Heat the oil in a saucepan over medium heat and cook the onion until golden. Add the chopped garlic and cook for about 3 minutes. Add the beans, salt and chilli, if using, and cook, without stirring, for 5 minutes. Now stir until the onion is dispersed right through the beans. If it is too dry, add 125 ml (4 fl oz/½ cup) of water. Cover with a lid, reduce the heat to low and simmer for 1 hour, stirring every 10 minutes or so. After 50 minutes, add the tomato, whole garlic cloves, cumin and pepper, if using, and cook for the final 10 minutes. This is ideal served with Boiled rice with egg noodles (see page 36).

Note: My mum only uses one 'hot' ingredient in this casserole—either chilli or pepper, not both.

Fasolia otah
Vegetarian baked bean casserole
serves 6–8

400 g (14 oz/2 cups) dried borlotti
   beans
4 tablespoons olive oil
4 onions, roughly chopped
1 red capsicum (pepper), seeded
   and chopped
6 garlic cloves, roughly chopped
1 long red chilli, seeded and chopped
6 soft cooking tomatoes, blanched,
   peeled and diced
1 tablespoon basil, finely chopped
1 teaspoon ground cumin
¼ teaspoon ground cinnamon
salt
2 tablespoons tomato paste
   (concentrated purée)

Soak the beans in water overnight. Rinse and drain.

Boil the beans in 1 litre (35 fl oz/4 cups) of water over high heat. Once the water boils, reduce the heat, cover with the lid, then simmer for 1 hour or until the beans soften.

In a separate saucepan, heat the oil and cook the onion over low heat until it begins to soften. Stir in the capsicum and cook for about 1 minute. Add the garlic, chilli, tomato, basil, cumin, cinnamon, and some salt and cook for about 20 minutes, stirring occasionally.

Strain the beans in a colander. Add the beans to the pan with the vegetables. Mix 125 ml (4 fl oz/½ cup) of hot water with the tomato paste, add to the saucepan and stir to combine. Bring to the boil over high heat. Reduce the heat and simmer for 20 minutes, covered with a lid. Season to taste. This is ideal served with Boiled rice with egg noodles (see page 36).

Yakn't
Lamb shank and potato casserole

serves 4

vegetable oil, for cooking

4 lamb shanks

40 g (1½ oz) butter

2 onions, chopped

½ garlic bulb, cloves separated
and peeled

1 teaspoon my family's baharat spice
mix (see page 22)

1 teaspoon salt

6 potatoes, washed, peeled and diced

125 g (4½ oz/½ cup) tomato paste
(concentrated purée)

Heat a large saucepan over high heat, add a little oil and sear the lamb shanks until brown. Remove from the pan.

Reduce the heat to low, melt the butter and cook the onion until soft. Add the garlic, baharat and salt and mix well. Pour 3 litres (105 fl oz/12 cups) of water into the pan and bring to the boil. Simmer, covered, for 1 hour or until the lamb is tender, then add the potato and tomato paste and cook for a further 30 minutes. Season to taste. This is ideal served with Boiled rice with egg noodles (see page 36).

Fassoulia
White bean casserole

serves 6

400 g (14 oz/2 cups) dried white beans,
such as white kidney beans or
cannellini beans

vegetable oil, for frying

8 pieces lamb neck, bone in

3 onions, roughly chopped

10 garlic cloves, crushed

2 small potatoes, cubed

2 tablespoons tomato paste
(concentrated purée)

½ teaspoon salt

Soak the beans overnight. Rinse and drain.

Heat a saucepan over high heat, add a little oil and sear the meat, in batches, if necessary, until browned. Remove from the pan. Reduce the heat to low, add the onion and garlic and cook until softened. Add the beans and meat and 3 litres (105 fl oz/12 cups) of water and bring to the boil. Reduce the heat to very low heat, add the potato, cover and simmer for 2 hours, or until the meat is tender. About 10 minutes before you remove the pan from the heat, stir in the tomato paste and salt. This is ideal served with Boiled rice with egg noodles (see page 36).

Spenegh

English spinach and beef casserole

serves 6–8

This is a very delicate dish to cook—everything has to be added at the right time. The ingredients need to be handled with care once they are added to the pan.

3 bunches English spinach
4 tablespoons pine nuts
50 g (1¾ oz) butter
2 onions, chopped
500 g (1 lb 2 oz) diced beef
   (chuck steak)
1 cinnamon stick
5 garlic cloves, crushed
1 teaspoon finely chopped coriander
   (cilantro)
5 soft cooking tomatoes, blanched,
   peeled and diced
3 tablespoons lemon juice
2 teaspoons salt

Wash the spinach thoroughly. Discard the stems and roughly chop the leaves.

Toast the pine nuts in a dry frying pan until they are golden. Set aside.

Heat the butter in a saucepan over medium heat, add the onion and cook until softened. Add the meat and cinnamon stick and cook for about 10 minutes—browning the meat on the outside will make this dish more flavoursome. Stir in the garlic, coriander, half of the tomato and 125 ml (4 fl oz/½ cup) of water and cover with a lid. Reduce the heat to low and cook for 30 minutes.

Add the spinach, pine nuts and remaining tomato, making sure they sit at the top. Cover and simmer for 15 minutes. About 3 minutes before you turn the heat off, gently stir in the lemon juice and salt and cover with the lid again. Turn the heat off and allow to rest for 10 minutes. This is ideal served with Boiled rice with egg noodles (see page 36).

Bemeh otah
Vegetarian okra casserole

serves 6

1 kg (2 lb 4 oz) okra
4 tablespoons olive oil
2 tablespoons vegetable oil
3 onions, chopped
8 garlic cloves, sliced
2 long red chillies, seeded and sliced
4 soft cooking tomatoes, blanched,
   peeled and diced
1 small handful coriander (cilantro),
   roughly chopped
1 teaspoon ground cumin
salt

Wash the okra thoroughly, then dry it completely by wrapping in a kitchen towel and gently pressing. Gently remove the stems by scraping around the edge with a knife. Make sure not to cut too much off, otherwise it will ooze a gel-like liquid and become difficult to cook with.

Working in batches, heat the olive oil in a frying pan that is at least 30 cm (12 inches) in diameter and lay the okra neatly into the pan, lining them up side by side to fill the base. Cook the okra on each side until slightly softened. Remove from the pan and drain on either a flat strainer or on kitchen paper. Repeat with the remaining okra, adding more oil, if necessary.

Heat the vegetable oil in a saucepan over medium heat. Cook the onion until it begins to soften. Add the garlic and stir with the onion for about 1 minute. Stir in the chilli, tomato, coriander, cumin and some salt. Cook for about 20 minutes over low heat. Add the okra to the pan and gently stir. Simmer for a further 10 minutes with the lid on. This is ideal served with Boiled rice with egg noodles (see page 36).

Fasolia bi lahem

Borlotti bean and lamb casserole

serves 4–6

400 g (14 oz/2 cups) dried borlotti
  beans
4 tablespoons butter
4 onions, cut into chunky pieces
500 g (1 lb 2 oz) diced lamb shank
  meat
1 cinnamon stick
1 potato, peeled and diced
3 tablespoons tomato paste
  (concentrated purée)
6 garlic cloves, roughly chopped
⅛ teaspoon chilli powder, optional
1 teaspoon salt
½ teaspoon ground cumin
¼ teaspoon black pepper

Soak the borlotti beans in water overnight. Rinse and drain.

Melt the butter in a saucepan over medium heat and cook the onion until soft. Add the lamb and cinnamon stick and cook for about 5 minutes while stirring. Add 2 litres (70 fl oz/8 cups) of water (or enough to cover) to the pan, then add the beans and potato. Bring to the boil over high heat. Reduce the heat, cover with a lid and simmer for 1 hour. Once the beans are soft, add the tomato paste, garlic and chilli powder, if using. Stir, then cover with the lid to cook for a further 15 minutes over low heat, or until the meat is tender. Remove from the heat, season with the salt, cumin and pepper and stir. This is ideal served with Boiled rice with egg noodles (see page 36).

Loubyeah bi lahem

Green bean and lamb casserole

serves 6–8

1 kg (2 lb 4 oz) green beans

40 g (1½ oz) butter

3 onions, chopped

500 g (1 lb 2 oz) diced lamb
(preferably from the shoulder)

1 cinnamon stick or ¼ teaspoon
ground cinnamon

1 teaspoon salt

3 soft cooking tomatoes, blanched,
peeled and diced

2 tablespoons tomato paste
(concentrated purée)

6 garlic cloves, left whole

½ teaspoon ground cumin

½ teaspoon finely ground Lebanese
black pepper

Trim the beans then, depending on their size, break them into two or three pieces. Wash and drain them.

Heat the butter in a saucepan over medium heat and cook the onion until soft. Stir in the meat and cinnamon stick (if using ground cinnamon, this will be added later). Cook the meat until it browns. Add the beans, 500 ml (17 fl oz/2 cups) of boiling water, the salt and ground cinnamon (if using) and cook, without stirring, for 3 minutes. Now stir until the onion is dispersed right through the beans and meat. Cover the pan with a lid and cook for 10 minutes. Uncover and stir thoroughly checking that the beans have begun to soften.

Add the tomato, tomato paste, garlic, cumin and pepper. Reduce the heat to low, cover with the lid and simmer for about 15 minutes or until the beans are soft. This is ideal served with Boiled rice with egg noodles (see page 36).

M'nasleh
Vegetable casserole

serves 6–8

2 ripe eggplants (aubergines), choose ones that are past their best

4 tablespoons vegetable oil

4 onions, cut into 4 wedges

2 red capsicums (peppers), finely chopped

200 g (7 oz) mushrooms, sliced

4 dark green zucchini (courgettes), sliced

2–3 garlic cloves

½ teaspoon salt

4 soft cooking tomatoes, blanched, peeled and diced

1 small red chilli, seeded and chopped

1 teaspoon ground cumin

Preheat the oven to 180°C (350°F/Gas 4). Peel and dice the eggplants into 3 cm (1¼ inch) cubes. Grease a baking tray with some oil and bake the eggplant pieces for about 15 minutes, or until tender. Remove from the oven and set aside. Brush the eggplant with some oil.

Heat 2 tablespoons of the oil in a frying pan over medium heat and cook the onion until soft. Remove from the heat and set aside with the eggplant. Add the chopped capsicum to the pan and cook, stirring occasionally, until it begins to soften. Remove from the heat and add to the other cooked vegetables. Cook the mushrooms briefly, removing them before they become watery. Set aside with the other vegetables. Cook the zucchini on both sides, adding a little more oil, as necessary, then add to the rest of the vegetables.

Crush the garlic with a sprinkle of salt using a mortar and pestle.

Combine all the cooked vegetables and garlic in a saucepan or wok and gently mix together over low heat. Add the tomato, chilli, cumin and salt and gently mix through again. Cook for a further 5 minutes. This is ideal served with Boiled rice with egg noodles (see page 36).

Harisse

Simple lamb shank and barley casserole

serves 4

This is a very old recipe that is nutritious and filling. My great grandmother used to cook this dish for her ten children, seven boys and three girls. It's a dish that my mother has kept close to her heart because she learnt it from her grandmother.

20 g (¾ oz) butter
4 lamb shanks, meat removed
   and diced
1 cinnamon stick
440 g (15½ oz/2 cups) barley
salt and finely ground Lebanese black
   pepper

Melt the butter in a saucepan over medium heat, add the diced lamb and cook until browned.

Pour 2 litres (70 fl oz/8 cups) of water into the pan along with the cinnamon and barley. Bring to the boil, then reduce the heat to medium. Cook, stirring occasionally, for about 2 hours, or until the meat is tender and falling apart and the liquid is reduced and thickened. Season to taste.

Batata m'luheyeah
Shaved potato casserole
serves 4

4 tablespoons olive oil

3 onions, finely chopped

1 long red chilli, seeded and finely
   chopped or ¼ teaspoon chilli
   powder, optional

4 soft cooking tomatoes, blanched,
   peeled and diced

6 potatoes (preferably pontiac)

1½ teaspoons salt

In a saucepan, heat the oil over medium heat and sauté the onion until golden brown. If you are using fresh chilli cook it with the onion. Stir in the tomato, cover with the lid and allow to cook for 10 minutes. Keep an eye on the tomato and stir occasionally.

Meanwhile, peel the potatoes and soak in a bowl with enough cold water to cover. Slice each potato as thinly as possible with either a knife or a peeler to about 2 mm (1/16 inch) thick, then return to the bowl while you do the rest. Transfer the potato to a colander and wash.

Add the thin slices of potato to the pan with the onion and stir over high heat. Cover with a lid and stir occasionally until it begins to boil. Reduce the heat to medium and check after 10 minutes to see if the potatoes have started to soften. Reduce the heat to low (if you are using chilli powder, add it now), add the salt and simmer for 20 minutes, or until the potatoes are soft. Serve as a main meal with salads, labneh (see page 31) and Boiled rice with egg noodles (see page 36).

Bazella ma'a rooz
Lamb and pea casserole

serves 4–6

40 g (1½ oz) butter

3 brown onions, chopped

5 garlic cloves, chopped

500 g (1 lb 2 oz) diced lamb

500 g (1 lb 2 oz/3¼ cups) shelled peas
  (see Note)

1 carrot, finely chopped

4 soft cooking tomatoes, blanched,
  peeled and roughly chopped

1 teaspoon salt

1 cinnamon stick

1 bay leaf

Heat the butter in a saucepan over medium–low heat and cook the onion and garlic until soft. Add the meat and stir. When the meat is cooked, stir in the peas and carrot. Once the peas and carrot begin to soften, add the tomato, then stir. Add 1 litre (35 fl oz/4 cups) of water, the salt, cinnamon stick and bay leaf. Bring to the boil, then reduce the heat to low. Partially cover with a lid and simmer for 1 hour. Season to taste. This is ideal served with Boiled rice with egg noodles (see page 36).

Note: You need to buy about 1.3 kg (3 lb) of peas in the pods to get 500 g (1 lb 2 oz) shelled peas. If you don't have fresh peas, you can use frozen.

Rooshta

Bean and home-made pasta soup

serves 6

My mother was taught this age-old recipe by her grandmother. Rooshta can be made with either borlotti beans or brown lentils.

300 g (10½ oz/1½ cups) dried borlotti
    beans or 280 g (10 oz/1½ cups)
    brown lentils
125 ml (4 fl oz/½ cup) vegetable oil
3 onions, chopped
1 teaspoon salt
500 g (1 lb 2 oz) plain (all-purpose)
    flour, plus extra, as required

If you are using borlotti beans, soak them in water overnight.

Drain the beans or, if using lentils, wash them thoroughly and rummage through to see if there are any stones.

Heat the oil in a large saucepan over high heat and add the onion. Sauté the onion until brown, stirring occasionally. Add 3 litres (105 fl oz/12 cups) of water, the beans or lentils and half the salt and boil, partially covered for about 1 hour, or until the beans or lentils are soft.

Meanwhile, to make the pasta dough, put the flour, remaining salt and 250 ml (9 fl oz/1 cup) of warm water in a large bowl and knead to make a dough. Allow to rest for 5 minutes. Have extra flour by your side to sprinkle onto the dough, if required. Sprinkle some flour onto a flat work surface. Use a rolling pin to roll out the dough to about 5 mm (¼ inch) thick. Sprinkle flour on the top of the dough and spread it to cover. Roll up the dough as if making a tight wrap. Cut about 5 mm (¼ inch) thick slices along the rolled-up dough. Each slice should be a swirl of dough (looks like thick fettuccine when you unroll it).

Once the beans or lentils are cooked, ensure the water is boiling rapidly over high heat and drop the dough into the pan. Continue cooking for 10 minutes, stirring occasionally, until the pasta is cooked. Remove the pan from the heat and season to taste.

Mahloota
Mixed bean soup
serves 8

100 g (3½ oz/½ cup) dried borlotti
   beans
110 g (3¾ oz/½ cup) dried chickpeas
95 g (3¼ oz/½ cup) brown lentils
110 g (3¾ oz/½ cup) barley
2 tablespoons olive oil
3 onions, chopped
1 bunch silverbeet (Swiss chard),
   stems removed, leaves shredded
   (see Note)
salt

Combine the beans, chickpeas, lentils and barley in a large strainer and wash thoroughly under running water. Transfer to a bowl, cover with water and soak overnight. Drain.

Place the beans, chickpeas, lentils and barley in a saucepan, add 4 litres (140 fl oz/16 cups) of water, cover with a lid and bring to the boil over medium heat. Once boiled, reduce the heat to low.

Heat the oil in a frying pan and cook the onion over low–medium heat until golden brown. Add the onion to the beans. Reduce the heat to low and simmer for 1½–2 hours. Check the water level occasionally—if the water has reduced and the beans are drying out, add about 500 ml (17 fl oz/2 cups) of boiling water.

Once the beans have cooked, add the silverbeet and salt to taste and cook for a further 10 minutes.

Note: If you can't find silverbeet, you can use 2 bunches of English spinach instead.

Aads bi hamod
Silverbeet and lentil soup

serves 8

Mum loves her garlic and her onions because 'it brings out the flavour'. Begin with 6 or 8 garlic cloves and work your way up (mum uses a whole bulb).

555 g (1 lb 4 oz/3 cups) brown lentils

2–3 brown onions, finely chopped

1 large potato, peeled and diced into 2 cm (¾ inch) cubes

6–8 garlic cloves, or to taste

1 teaspoon salt, or to taste

4 tablespoons olive oil

500 g (1 lb 2 oz/½ bunch) silverbeet (Swiss chard)

lemon wedges, parmesan cheese shavings and Tabasco, to serve, optional

Wash the lentils thoroughly and rummage through to see if there are any stones.

In a large saucepan combine 3.5 litres (122 fl oz/14 cups) of water, the lentils, onion and diced potato. Bring to the boil over high heat.

Crush the garlic with a sprinkle of salt using a mortar and pestle. Mix the oil with the garlic, then add to the pan and stir into the boiling water. Reduce the heat to low, cover slightly with a lid and cook for 30 minutes, stirring occasionally. Stirring will allow the oil to disperse right through, instead of sitting at the top.

Wash the silverbeet and discard the thick stems. Wrap your hand around the leafy bunch and chop the leaves into rough 1.5–2 cm (⅝–¾ inch) chunks.

Once the lentils have softened, add the silverbeet to the boiling water. Stir in the silverbeet, cover with the lid and simmer for 20 minutes before you turn off the heat. Season with salt and stand for about 10 minutes before you serve.

This soup can be sipped hot or cold. Lemon can be added to the individual serves. Feel free to have a bit of fun with this soup when you serve it—shavings of parmesan cheese add another dimension to the taste, as does Tabasco sauce.

Note: The next day the flavour of the soup is more concentrated and you can really taste the silverbeet.

Joumana's shawarba
Joumana's vegetable soup
serves 6–8

Stock
2 celery stalks, chopped
2 carrots, peeled and chopped
2 zucchini (courgettes), chopped
1 corn, halved
1 onion, chopped
3 garlic cloves, chopped
½ red capsicum (pepper), chopped
2 soft cooking tomatoes, diced
1 cinnamon stick

Soup
200 g (7 oz/1 cup) soup mix
2 carrots, chopped
1 corn, kernels sliced off the cob
1 onion, chopped
3 garlic cloves, chopped
2 zucchini (courgettes), chopped
1 head broccoli, florets separated
5 soft cooking tomatoes, blended
   in a food processor
salt and finely ground Lebanese black
   pepper
1 small handful flat-leaf (Italian)
   parsley

Soak the soup mix in water overnight. Rinse and drain.

To make the stock, simmer all the ingredients in a saucepan filled with 3 litres (105 fl oz/12 cups) of water for 1 hour. Strain, reserving the liquid.

Return the stock to a clean pan. Add the soup mix, bring to the boil and then simmer for 30 minutes, covered, over low heat. Add the carrot, corn, onion and garlic and simmer for 20 minutes, covered, then add the zucchini, broccoli and tomatoes. Bring back to the boil, then simmer for 10 minutes. Season to taste, stir through the parsley and serve.

Pickling *and* Preserving

Citi Leila may have left the demands of the village life behind her in Lebanon but she can't help herself from pickling and preserving some of our favourite condiments. Rows of glass jars filled with pickled olives, stuffed eggplant (aubergine), green beans, turnips and cucumber, to name a few, are stocked in a designated cupboard in her kitchen. In her fridge are the usual array of jams including apricot, fig and apple along with a surprise or two based on a new fruit variety she has experimented with and turned into a jam.

I love when Citi and her daughters recall their childhood experiences of life in the village. As a child I remember these stories playing back in my mind like a fairytale of a time and place so far away from my own reality...

'At the end of every summer in the village, the whole community worked hard together to prepare the abundance of fresh crops for storage to last throughout the winter,' Citi explains.

Almost every vegetable had to be picked and placed on special thick cotton sheets under the sun for a couple of days. When they were completely sun-dried or when there was no more moisture left, they were packed and stored away to be consumed throughout winter. Sun-dried corn was either turned into cornflour or left as shrivelled dry kernels to add to winter soups. Citi had to pick the zucchini (courgettes), wash and then drench them with salt before surrendering their moisture to the sun. The dry zucchini were then sealed tightly in glass jars with pickling solution made from water and salt and stored in a dark place. Vine leaves were also pickled in jars with the same solution. Long necklaces of haricot, romano and borlotti beans were individually sewn with a needle and a double layer of cotton thread and then hung out to dry. The sun-dried tomatoes were also painstakingly threaded into very long necklaces that hung in the kitchen along with the beans for easy

access. 'There was no such thing as a freezer,' Citi explains, 'I had hundreds of jars piled up as well as huge containers that I stored in a dark cool place in our not so big house'.

Before Gidi left for Australia he sold all of the family's livestock except for one goat. 'Our over-utilised pet,' as Citi often likes to call it. She explains, 'Before winter I would milk it really well to make enough pickled labneh balls and loose cheese to get us through'. Her fruit jams were treated as winter desserts and almost every fruit was turned into a sweet delight. 'The children's favourite dessert was the pears and apples that I dipped in atter,' Citi explains. Atter is the solution of boiling syrup made from sugar and water and Citi would dip the fruit into this mixture to create wonderful sugary treats. The fruit would then sit in the jars filled with the sugared syrup all winter to be enjoyed by the kids. This was deemed the special dessert, which was served to her sweet-toothed children only during the most desperate chills of winter when they had been locked inside by the snow for days.

The taste of pickled green olives will always transport me back to when I was a young girl and I was given the task of helping Citi pickle the olives. There was a mammoth amount of green olives to get through—these were then split between the families and preserved in jars to be eaten throughout the year as part of mezze. One of the perks of being the eldest grandchild is that I was involved in the family preparations as much as possible. Citi and I would both be sitting companionably at her work table, which she had hammered together with scrap pieces of wood. All around us would be boxes and boxes of green olives. Each individual olive had to be placed on the table and then gently crushed with the base of a glass cup until it formed a crack. It was then thrown into a huge tub of water. Once we had crushed our way through the hundreds and hundreds of olives that stained our hands to a blood clot purple, we left them in a pool of fresh cold water to soak overnight. The next day the olives were put in jars and on their way to becoming pickled.

Khiyaar makboos
Pickled cucumber
fills a 2 litre (70 fl oz) jar

90 g (3¼ oz/⅔ cup) fine sea salt
1.5 kg (3 lb 5 oz) small, thin Lebanese
    (short) cucumbers
1 small red chilli
2 garlic cloves, peeled and halved
250 ml (9 fl oz/1 cup) white vinegar

To make the brine, boil 2 litres (70 fl oz/8 cups) of water and the salt in a saucepan for 30 minutes. Set aside overnight.

Wash the cucumbers and place them in a 2 litre (70 fl oz/ 8 cup) sterilised glass jar. Add the chilli and garlic, cover with the vinegar, then top up with the brine. Loosely place the lid on the jar and leave overnight, then tighten the lid the next day. Store for 2 weeks before you open and eat.

Note: These will last for a year in a cool, dark place as long as they remain covered by brine.

Arnabiit makboos
Pickled cauliflower
fills a 2 litre (70 fl oz) jar

110 g (3¾ oz/½ cup) fine sea salt
1 head cauliflower, florets separated
1 beetroot (beet), peeled and cubed
2 garlic cloves, peeled
2 long red or green chillies, pierced
    with a needle
500 ml (17 fl oz/2 cups) white vinegar

To make the brine, boil 1.5 litres (52 fl oz/6 cups) water and the salt in a saucepan for 30 minutes. Set aside to cool overnight.

Put the cauliflower in a large saucepan, cover with water and bring to the boil. Remove from the heat. Strain and cool.

Fill a 2 litre (70 fl oz/8 cup) sterilised glass jar with the cauliflower, beetroot, garlic and chilli. Add the vinegar and enough of the brine to cover the cauliflower. Loosely place the lid on the jar overnight and tighten the lid the next day. Store for 2 weeks before you open and eat.

Note: These will last for a year in a cool, dark place as long as they remain covered by brine.

Baadhinjaan makboos
Pickled eggplant

fills a 2 litre (70 fl oz) jar

Pickled eggplant tastes great with meat. I love to wrap it in salad leaves, such as rocket (arugula), spinach or lettuce—one small piece is packed with flavour. It's also great cut into pieces and served with cheese and crackers.

1.5 kg (3 lb 5 oz) small round black
   eggplants (aubergines)
1 tablespoon fine sea salt, plus extra,
   for sprinkling
8 garlic cloves
2 long red chillies
150 g (5½ oz/1½ cups) walnuts
olive oil, to cover the eggplant

Remove the stems from the eggplants and wash.

Boil 2 litres (70 fl oz/8 cups) of water in a large saucepan with the salt. Cook the eggplants, in batches, in the salty boiling water for 2 minutes per batch. Remove the eggplants from the water and place in a strainer sitting over a bowl. Apply pressure to the eggplants to drain the fluid. Citi does this by covering the eggplant with a flat plate, then covering it with a kitchen towel followed by 2 bricks on top. Mum places bottles filled with liquid on top of the eggplant. Leave to drain, weighted, overnight in the refrigerator.

To make the stuffing, place the garlic and chillies in a food processor and pulse three times. Add the walnuts and pulse twice more. Transfer to a bowl.

Slit the eggplants lengthways to create an opening, just wide and deep enough to fill with stuffing. Pack each pocket tightly with stuffing (it can be useful to wear gloves as the chilli is hot). Place the eggplants in neat rows in a 2 litre (70 fl oz/8 cup) sterilised glass jar. Sprinkle a pinch of sea salt on every second layer. The eggplants should be compact, pushed firmly towards the bottom of the jar.

Tip the jar upside down onto a tray and prop it slightly up to enable the excess fluid to drain out overnight.

Turn the jar upright and fill it with olive oil to cover. Loosely place the lid on the jar and leave overnight, then tighten the lid the next day. Store for 2 weeks before you open and eat.

Note: These will last for a year in a cool, dark place as long as they remain covered by oil.

Loubyeah makbooseh
Pickled green beans
fills a 1 litre (35 fl oz) jar

3 garlic cloves

2 tablespoons fine sea salt, plus extra,
   for sprinkling

750 g (1 lb 10 oz) green beans, trimmed

375 ml (13 fl oz/1½ cups) extra virgin
   olive oil, to cover the beans

Lightly crush the garlic with a sprinkle of salt using a mortar and pestle.

Boil 2 litres (70 fl oz/8 cups) of water in a saucepan with the rest of the sea salt. Blanch the beans for 3 minutes in the boiling water. Remove the beans from the water and strain. Set the beans aside and allow to cool. Transfer the beans to a bowl, add the garlic and toss.

Place the beans in a 1 litre (35 fl oz/4 cup) sterilised glass jar. Fill the jar with olive to cover the beans. Loosely place the lid on the jar and leave overnight, then tighten the lid the next day. Store for 3 weeks before opening.

Note: These will last for a year in a cool, dark place as long as they remain covered by oil.

Zaytoon makboos
Pickled green olives
fills a 1 litre (35 fl oz) jar

In my family, we make sure that we have at least one companion alongside when we are pickling olives—there are many boxes to get through and an extra pair of hands makes all the difference.

500 g (1 lb 2 oz) raw green olives
220 g (7¾ oz/1 cup) fine sea salt, plus
  1 tablespoon sea salt, extra
185 ml (6 fl oz/¾ cup) olive oil
6 small red chillies, stems removed
3 fresh lemon leaves, washed and
  cut in half
2 lemons, cut into quarters

Fill a large bowl or bucket with water. Using a pestle, gently put pressure on the olives to create a crack in the skin, then drop them into the water as you crush them. Soak in cold water overnight.

To make the brine, boil 2 litres (70 fl oz/8 cups) water and the salt in a saucepan for 30 minutes. Set aside to cool the liquid overnight.

Drain the water from the olives. In a large bowl, mix the olives with the oil, extra salt, chillies, lemon leaves and lemon quarters. Tightly squeeze each handful of the olives towards the bottom of a 1 litre (35 fl oz/4 cup) sterilised glass jar. The olives should be be very compact. Pour the remaining oil mixture into the jar. Fill the jar with enough brine to cover the olives. Loosely place the lid on the jar and leave overnight, then tighten the lid the next day. Store for 2 weeks before you open and eat.

Note: These will last for a year in the fridge as long as they remain covered by brine.

Lift makboos

Pickled turnips

fills a 1 litre (35 fl oz) jar

2 tablespoons fine sea salt

2 turnips, washed thoroughly and cut into thick slices

½ beetroot (beet), peeled and cubed

2 garlic cloves, halved

250 ml (9 fl oz/1 cup) white vinegar

To make the brine, boil 1 litre (35 fl oz/4 cups) of water and 1 tablespoon of the sea salt in a saucepan for about 30 minutes. Set aside to cool overnight. Soak the turnips in a separate batch of cold water with the remaining salt overnight.

Drain the turnips. In a bowl mix the turnips with the beetroot and garlic.

Fill a 1 litre (35 fl oz/4 cup) sterilised glass jar with the turnip, beetroot and garlic. Add the vinegar and enough brine to cover. Loosely place the lid on the jar and leave overnight, then tighten the lid the next day. Store for 2 weeks before you open and eat.

Note: The pickled turnips will last for a year in a cool, dark place. The beetroot provides colour to the turnips but is not meant to be eaten.

My mother's old-fashioned way of testing for the right pickling solution:

'To know if you have enough salt, experiment by adding salt to water. Place an egg in the water. If the egg rises, you have enough salt and the perfect pickling solution.'

Labneh makbooseh
Marinated labneh balls
makes 18 balls

If you don't like chilli, you can make the pickled labneh balls without it.

2 tablespoons fine sea salt
2 litres (70 fl oz/8 cups) laben that
    has been in the fridge for 2 days
    (see page 30)
¼ teaspoon chilli powder
3¼ tablespoons paprika
500 ml (17 fl oz/2 cups) extra virgin
    olive oil

Mix the salt through the laben. Pour the laben into a cotton sack (similar to a pillow case) or piece of muslin (cheesecloth) and drain out the fluid by either hanging it outside (if the weather is moderate, hang in the shade away from direct sunlight) or in a strainer suspended over a bowl in the fridge. Drain in the sack for 3 days. Throw out the build up of liquid in the bowl each day.

On the third day the laben should be hard enough to roll into labneh balls. Place the labneh in a bowl and mix through the chilli powder and 1 teaspoon of the paprika.

Make sure that you are not in direct sunlight when making the labneh balls. Scoop out about 1 tablespoon of labneh. Roll into a ball between the palms of your hands. Moisten your palms with a little olive oil if the labneh is sticky. Cover a flat surface with the remaining paprika. Roll the balls one at a time in the paprika to coat.

Pour some of the olive oil into a 2 litre (70 fl oz/8 cup) capacity sterilised glass jar and drop the paprika-covered labneh balls in it. Top up with the remaining olive oil. Place the lid on the jar. Keep in the fridge for 1 week before opening.

Note: These will last for a year in the fridge as long as they remain covered by oil.

3
Joumana
Lessons in Hospitality

The Rituals of Welcome

'Guests are always welcome and it is very important that they are welcomed with warmth and whole heartedness as soon as they are at your door. They are entering your space and as the host it is up to you to provide an enjoyable experience for them.' My mother, Joumana

'Ahlan wa sahlan' are the words of welcome that all guests are greeted with the moment they enter the family home. A solid handshake is followed by three kisses, alternating between cheeks. Now they are in the hospitable hands of the host. Like most Lebanese families, my mother's home is welcoming and decorated in a way that uses the available space to share with extended family and friends. Entertaining is central to our way of life, and the finest crockery, cutlery and utensils are always used for guests.

When I was growing up, any guests who came to visit were ushered directly into the formal lounge area. This space was strictly off limits for us kids, even when the couches in the television room (or the informal lounge room as it was known) had to be replaced and we sat on milk crates for weeks. Mum adored her plush watermelon-coloured velvet couches that filled the formal lounge to create an inviting U-shape. The couches were of her own design and she even had the legs of the three small serving tables made to match the elaborate wooden carvings of the legs and frames of her beloved couches.

We had a big backyard with an equal concrete-to-grass ratio, as they were both equally important. The grass was to accommodate the precious vegetable patch and the concrete was for the kids to play on.

There was always something on. If it wasn't the barbecue sizzling away on a glorious sunny day, it was an indoor feast. Visits were never planned or booked, but always expected and welcomed. As a child, weekend recreational activities usually took place at either a cousin's house or the family home. Growing up with an abundance of cousins of a similar age meant that we had enough kids to make up competitive sports teams. The weekend was an opportunity for families to catch up in the comfort of each other's homes. Day-long visits were filled with conversation, cooking and eating together, often late into the evening.

We had a doorbell that was fit for an army drill. Every time it was pressed it startled me. I never did get used to it. On the other hand, Mum's face would brighten up with anticipation. She had always been a great entertainer. 'I love opening my house to family and friends,' she says. Even school friends who ran away from their own homes sought refuge here. Mum laughs at the memory of how we used to called it 'the half-way house'. She always listened to the kids' stories and, when she fed them, their faces glowed as they succumbed to her love. Mum is capable of translating her love and nurturing nature into flavours.

Fuelled by the philosophy of 'the early-bird catches the worm', Mum usually did her fresh food and produce shopping early on Saturday mornings. She still doesn't believe in weekend sleep-ins. 'Why should I waste my time getting stuck in all sorts of weekend traffic when I could be with my family instead,' she has always argued.

She always took great pleasure in greeting the butcher first thing in the morning as she waited for him

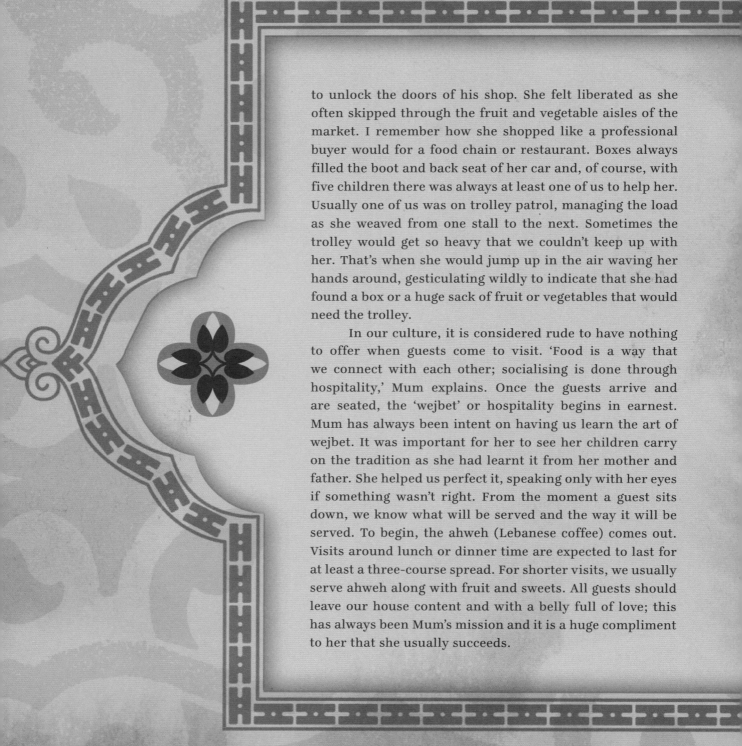

to unlock the doors of his shop. She felt liberated as she often skipped through the fruit and vegetable aisles of the market. I remember how she shopped like a professional buyer would for a food chain or restaurant. Boxes always filled the boot and back seat of her car and, of course, with five children there was always at least one of us to help her. Usually one of us was on trolley patrol, managing the load as she weaved from one stall to the next. Sometimes the trolley would get so heavy that we couldn't keep up with her. That's when she would jump up in the air waving her hands around, gesticulating wildly to indicate that she had found a box or a huge sack of fruit or vegetables that would need the trolley.

In our culture, it is considered rude to have nothing to offer when guests come to visit. 'Food is a way that we connect with each other; socialising is done through hospitality,' Mum explains. Once the guests arrive and are seated, the 'wejbet' or hospitality begins in earnest. Mum has always been intent on having us learn the art of wejbet. It was important for her to see her children carry on the tradition as she had learnt it from her mother and father. She helped us perfect it, speaking only with her eyes if something wasn't right. From the moment a guest sits down, we know what will be served and the way it will be served. To begin, the ahweh (Lebanese coffee) comes out. Visits around lunch or dinner time are expected to last for at least a three-course spread. For shorter visits, we usually serve ahweh along with fruit and sweets. All guests should leave our house content and with a belly full of love; this has always been Mum's mission and it is a huge compliment to her that she usually succeeds.

The Banquet

When the coffee has been drunk, it is time for the mezze. When we were young, that's when mum would catch our eyes to remind us that we were up to the next stage in the proceedings. The mezze is usually served in the formal lounge room before the main meal. A mosaic-like spread of small bowls and platters filled with nuts, chopped vegetables, pickles and dips is brought out to be shared. I remember as a child the array of pistachios, walnuts, shelled pumpkin seeds, almonds and cashew nuts that were stored in long green plastic containers and they never seemed to be empty or run out. If Mum was well prepared, she would soak carrot, celery sticks and almonds in water and keep them in the fridge. The cold moist texture was a real treat in summer. Sometimes we served pickled turnips and cucumber instead of chopped fresh vegetables to dip into the labeh, hummous and babba ghanoush. The brave-hearted sip on arak (an aniseed-flavoured alcoholic drink) served in small shot glasses filled with ice and water. Juices and soft drinks are always offered as well.

The Feast

'Id fadaloo' is the term used to welcome the guests to the dining table for the main meal—a banquet of tantalising dishes prepared by the women. When it is time to start cooking, the women are magnetically drawn to the kitchen. Although Mum's kitchen is her domain, female cousins and friends comfortably join in for these cook-offs. There is something special about the way the women work together, respecting each other's space, connecting with each other through their cooking.

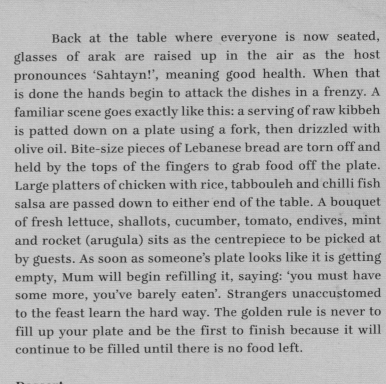

Back at the table where everyone is now seated, glasses of arak are raised up in the air as the host pronounces 'Sahtayn!', meaning good health. When that is done the hands begin to attack the dishes in a frenzy. A familiar scene goes exactly like this: a serving of raw kibbeh is patted down on a plate using a fork, then drizzled with olive oil. Bite-size pieces of Lebanese bread are torn off and held by the tops of the fingers to grab food off the plate. Large platters of chicken with rice, tabbouleh and chilli fish salsa are passed down to either end of the table. A bouquet of fresh lettuce, shallots, cucumber, tomato, endives, mint and rocket (arugula) sits as the centrepiece to be picked at by guests. As soon as someone's plate looks like it is getting empty, Mum will begin refilling it, saying: 'you must have some more, you've barely eaten'. Strangers unaccustomed to the feast learn the hard way. The golden rule is never to fill up your plate and be the first to finish because it will continue to be filled until there is no food left.

Dessert

The final stage of the wejbet is the serving of dessert, tea and coffee that usually takes place back in the formal lounge. When I was young, Mum would win the hearts of her nieces and nephews by making them a special dessert treat. She usually whipped up a large tray of knefeh from scratch when she ran out of other sweets to offer. Knefeh is basically made by boiling semolina with milk and cream. It is then poured over a thin layer of cornflake crumbs that cover the bottom of a baking tray. More of the crumbs are sprinkled on top of the cream. It is then baked for a few minutes. While the knefeh was baking, Mum usually

◆ **Lessons in Hospitality**

prepared the attar (sugar syrup) that we liked to pour over our serve of knefeh when it was piping hot. Desserts such as this along with a platter of seasonal fruits are always served with either cafe blanc (tea) or another round of Lebanese coffee. A few drops of either orange blossom or rosewater are added to boiling water to make cafe blanc, which is served as a digestive.

When I went to Lebanon a few years ago, I saw just how important socialising and connecting with the community is to everyday life in my parents' homeland. I spent the summer break there while the children were on school holidays. It was a time when most of the villagers who abandoned their homes in winter to take up residence in cities such as Beirut returned to Becharee to enjoy the relaxed atmosphere of the mountains. Their verandahs are traditionally huge and look out onto the street so that the residents are able to invite in neighbours who pass by their house. Lebanese coffee brews all day long and cups are sipped between meals. The children also engage with the adults as the conversations are open to anyone—just like the hospitality.

Kofta nayee

Raw kofta

serves 6–8

1 kg (2 lb 4 oz) diced lamb shoulder (make sure it is ultra fresh if you are serving this raw)

½ large handful flat-leaf (Italian) parsley, chopped

2 onions, finely chopped

1 teaspoon finely ground Lebanese black pepper

1 teaspoon ground cumin

1 long red or green chilli (seeded, optional), chopped, or ¼ teaspoon chilli powder

1½ teaspoons salt

sliced spring onion (scallion), radish, mint leaves and sliced chilli, to serve

Combine all the ingredients in a bowl and mix together with your hands. Place two handfuls of the mixture in a food processor and pulse about three times. Unlike the soft creamy kibbeh, the texture of kofta is coarse. Once all the mixture has been pulsed, return to the bowl and mix to combine.

To serve, shape the kofta into a neat round on a plate and garnish with spring onion, radish, mint and chilli. This also goes well with many bitter greens, such as witlof (chicory/Belgian endive), watercress and large rocket (aruula) leaves.

Raw kofta should only be eaten fresh on the day that it is made. After that the remaining mixture is used to make flat or finger patties, casserole dishes or home-made kofta pizza.

Flat patties: Make flat patties about 7 cm (2¾ inches) in diameter and 1 cm (¾ inch) thick by patting the kofta into shape with your hands. As you are moulding the patty, moisten your hand with water. The patties can be pan-fried in a frying pan coated with a tiny amount of oil. Alternatively, they can be grilled (broiled), baked or barbecued by brushing the patties with oil first.

Finger patties: Finger patties are cooked exactly the same way as flat patties but shaped differently. Dampen your hands with water and roll a small amount of kofta into a sausage shape as long as the width of your hand, then gently press to flatten slightly.

Home-made kofta pizza: Preheat a grill (broiler) to high. Spread a thin layer of the raw kofta on Lebanese bread and grill until the meat begins to brown. Remove the pizza from the grill and top with sliced tomato, olives, onion and a sprinkle of cheese. Place the pizza back under the grill and cook until the topping is cooked and the cheese is melted. This can also be made in the oven. Go crazy with the toppings and experiment with your favourite combinations.

Note: If you are cooking the kofta, you can use beef.

Kofta bi zoom
Kofta ball and vegetable casserole
serves 6–8

Kofta balls

1 kg (2 lb 4 oz) diced lamb shoulder
　or beef shoulder

½ bunch flat-leaf (Italian) parsley,
　chopped

2 onions, chopped

1 small handful mint, chopped

1 long red or green chilli

1 teaspoon finely ground Lebanese
　black pepper

1 teaspoon ground cinnamon

1 teaspoon ground cumin

1 teaspoon salt

3 tablespoons vegetable oil

2 onions, chopped

2 carrots, peeled and chopped

8 garlic cloves, finely chopped

1 kg (2 lb 4 oz) soft cooking tomatoes,
　blanched, peeled and diced

1 tablespoon tomato paste
　(concentrated purée)

To make the kofta balls, mix all the ingredients together and blend in a food processor until chopped and combined.

Roll the mixture into balls about 3 cm (1¼ inch) in diameter. Place the balls on a baking tray.

Heat 2 tablespoons of the oil in a non-stick saucepan over medium–high heat and cook the kofta balls in batches until browned. Set aside.

Reduce the heat to medium, add a little more oil, if necessary, and cook the onion for 5 minutes or until soft. Add the carrot and cook for 5 minutes; add the garlic and cook for 2 minutes. Return the kofta balls to the pan along with the tomato, tomato paste and enough water just to cover. Cover with a lid and bring to the boil over high heat. Reduce the heat and simmer, covered, for 25 minutes. Season to taste.

Kofta bi sayneeyeh
Baked kofta and vegetable stack

serves 6

If you prefer, you can use the recipe for raw kofta (see page 116) instead of the recipe given here. My aunts differ on how they like to cook their kofta: Aunty Hind likes to bake hers, while Aunty Rosa prefers to pan-fry hers before layering them.

Kofta

500 g (1 lb 2 oz) diced lamb shoulder
   or beef shoulder

1 large handful flat-leaf (Italian)
   parsley, chopped

1 onion, chopped

1 small handful mint, chopped

½ long fresh red or green chilli

½ teaspoon finely ground Lebanese
   black pepper

½ teaspoon ground cinnamon

½ teaspoon ground cumin

½ teaspoon salt

vegetable oil, for greasing

3 potatoes, sliced

3 onions, sliced into rings

1 teaspoon salt

1 teaspoon ground cumin

1 teaspoon finely ground Lebanese
   black pepper

1 red capsicum (pepper), seeded
   and thickly sliced

6 tomatoes, sliced

1 tablespoon tomato paste
   (concentrated purée)

35 g (1¼ oz) butter, thinly sliced

To make the kofta, mix all the ingredients together and blend in a food processor until chopped and combined.

Preheat the oven to 190°C (375°F/Gas 5). To mould the kofta mixture into flat patties, dampen your hands with some water. You should get about twelve 7 cm (2¾ inch) diameter patties.

Grease a frying pan with oil and heat over medium heat. Working in batches, sear the kofta on both sides until they are partially cooked. Remove the kofta patties from the heat and set aside. Leave any juices in the frying pan for cooking the vegetables. Cook the potato slices and onion rings separately in the pan until they are partially cooked, adding more oil as required. Remove from the pan and set aside separately.

Combine the salt, cumin and pepper in a small bowl—this will be your seasoning mixture.

In an oval 30 × 20 cm (12 × 8 inch) baking dish that is about 6 cm (2½ inches) high, layer the meat and vegetables, sprinkling with the seasoning mixture as you go. First, layer the base of the dish with half of the kofta patties, then all the potato, followed by a layer of the combined capsicum, onion and half the tomato slices. Top with the remaining patties and tomato slices.

Dissolve the tomato paste in 250 ml (9 fl oz/1 cup) of water and pour it over the top of the layered meat and vegetables. Sprinkle with the remaining seasoning mixture, then dot the butter over the top. Bake for 30 minutes, then loosely cover with foil and bake for a further 15 minutes or until the vegetables are tender. This is ideal served with Boiled rice with egg noodles (see page 36) or pasta.

Kibbeh nayee

Raw kibbeh

serves 6

Always use lean, fresh meat for kibbeh. You can either get your butcher to mince (grind) the meat or you can do it yourself. Either way, make sure the meat passes through the grinder three times. If you process the meat yourself, store it in the freezer for about 5 minutes before you start. The meat has to remain cold throughout the process of making this dish.

100 g (3½ oz/½ cup) fine crushed
·wheat (burghul)
500 g (1 lb 2 oz) lamb chunks (from
the leg, fat-free and ultra fresh)
mint leaves and radish, to serve
cold-pressed extra virgin olive oil, for
drizzling

Marhan
3 mint leaves, roughly chopped
2 basil leaves, roughly chopped
½ brown onion, roughly chopped
½ long red chilli, seeded and chopped,
or ¼ teaspoon chilli powder
½ teaspoon finely ground Lebanese
black pepper
1¼ teaspoons ground cumin or kibbeh
spice mix (see page 22)
1½ teaspoons salt

Fill a bowl with ice cubes and water. Wash the crushed wheat then soak in the iced water and leave in the freezer for about 15 minutes. Mince (grind) the meat three times. Put the meat in the freezer for 5 minutes.

To make the kibbeh, put the minced meat and 1 teaspoon of iced water in a food processor. Process until the meat is soft, finely processed and almost silky. Reserve about ¾ cup of the meat and chill the rest in the freezer until needed.

To make the marhan, put the ¾ cup meat and the rest of the ingredients in a food processor. Blend until creamy.

Drain the burghul, then squeeze it thoroughly. Add it to the marhan along with the meat from the freezer. Dip your hands in iced water, then knead the mixture thoroughly.

Kibbeh is traditionally served on an oval dish. The kibbeh is moulded into a mound. We usually decorate it by making an imprint along the sides and on the top with a knife. Garnish with mint and radish. If serving on a plate, drizzle with cold-pressed extra virgin olive oil and eat with Lebanese bread.

'The meat has to be ultra fresh, fat-free and vein-free.' Aunty Rosa

'For raw meat we use only lamb, preferably hogget. If we are going to cook it, we use either lamb or beef.' My mother, Joumana

Kibbeh *and* Kofta

In one of my earlier years of primary school, I had a female Egyptian teacher who came in once a week to interact with and instruct the students of Middle Eastern descent in order to teach us our language and history. As part of this class we learnt traditional Arabic songs. These songs were usually performed in front of the entire school for International Day along with other children from the various ethnic backgrounds that were represented at our school. It was an event held once a year by St. Brigid's Primary School in Marrickville, Sydney, to recognise and celebrate the diverse cultures of students and families that made up the school and, in a wider sense, the community at large.

On the day of the performance, our uniforms were swapped for colourful national costumes as we performed traditional dances and sang in different languages. Proud parents set up food stalls and produced dishes that represented their country of origin. I distinctly remember the aroma of culinary delights from around the world that swirled through the playground along with the myriad colours and sounds.

One year all the Middle Eastern children sang the *Kibbeh Song*, an ode to our national Lebanese dish. The song was accompanied by some simple hand gestures that mimicked the different techniques of cooking this significant Lebanese food. The basic words of the song are: '*Kibbeh, kibbeh, kibbitnah, heeyah illi rabitnah,*' which

translates as, 'Kibbeh is our dish and has been the vital source of our upbringing.'

Every time I make or eat kibbeh, this song plays in my head like a well-known jingle. I didn't think much of kibbeh back when I was performing the song to the rest of the school. In fact I didn't quite understand its significance at all. I would have unashamedly preferred to sing about my favourite meal at the time, which was marinated chicken wings doused in garlic sauce!

Kibbeh is basically made up of lean ground meat and burghul (crushed wheat). It is absolutely essential that the components remain cold throughout the preparation process. The marhan as my family calls it, is a blend of mint leaves, basil, onion, fresh chilli and seasoning. This is what gives the dish its distinct flavour. Huge quantities of this paste-like dish are usually made to form the basis of many different recipes that can be eaten raw, baked, barbecued or grilled (broiled).

The delicate process of making kibbeh and the resulting dish makes it the beautiful sister to kofta. Kofta is made tastier with a more fatty and coarse mince that has been blitzed through the food processor. It can also be eaten raw, baked, or made into a casserole. It is not as artfully versatile as kibbeh, which is moulded into different shapes and then stuffed and smoothed to perfection. Kofta is either made into patties, fingers (patties that are moulded into thick coils and slightly flattened), meatballs or Lebanese kofta pizza. Kibbeh and kofta are equally delicious in my view.

Kibbab

Kibbab ovals

makes 25

250 g (9 oz/1¼ cups) fine crushed
   wheat (burghul)
500 g (1 lb 2 oz) lean beef or lamb
   chunks

Marhan

3 mint leaves, roughly chopped
2 basil leaves, roughly chopped
½ brown onion, roughly chopped
½ long red chilli, seeded and chopped,
   or ¼ teaspoon chilli powder
½ teaspoon finely ground Lebanese
   black pepper
1¼ teaspoons ground cumin or kibbeh
   spice mix (see page 22)
1½ teaspoons salt

Hashweh (filling)

1 tablespoon vegetable oil, plus extra,
   for brushing
2 onions, finely chopped
250 g (9 oz) minced (ground) topside
   beef or lamb
125 g (4½ oz) butter
¼ teaspoon finely ground Lebanese
   black pepper
¼ teaspoon ground cumin
⅛ teaspoon chilli powder
⅛ teaspoon ground cinnamon
40 g (1½ oz/¼ cup) pine nuts, toasted

Preheat the oven to 200°C (400°F/Gas 6). Fill a bowl with ice cubes and water. Wash the crushed wheat then soak in the iced water and leave in the freezer for about 15 minutes. Mince (grind) the meat three times (or ask your butcher to do this for you). Put the meat in the freezer for 5 minutes.

To make the kibbeh, put the minced meat and 1 teaspoon of iced water in a food processor. Process until the meat is soft, finely processed and almost silky. Reserve about ¾ cup of the meat and chill the rest in the freezer until needed.

To make the marhan, put the ¾ cup meat and the rest of the ingredients in a food processor. Blend until creamy. Drain the burghul, then squeeze it thoroughly. Add it to the marhan along with the meat from the freezer. Dip your hands in iced water, then knead the mixture thoroughly.

To make the hashweh, heat the oil in a saucepan over low heat and cook the onion for about 10 minutes, or until soft. Remove from the pan and set aside in a bowl. Increase the heat to high, add the meat and cook until the juices have evaporated. Reduce the heat to low. Add the butter, pepper and spices and mix for 5 minutes, or until the meat is well cooked. Add to the bowl with the onion.

Brush two baking trays with oil.

Dampen your hands with some water and grab a handful of raw kibbeh. Mould it into an oval shape to fit in the palm of your hand. Wet your index finger and poke through the top of the oval. Make a hollow by working around the hole by pressing against the palm of your hand to create a thin wall. Place 1 tablespoon of the hashweh in the hole. Wet your hand and pinch the top together to seal. Roll between the palms of your hands into a neat torpedo shape.

Place the kibbab on the prepared trays, then brush the top with oil. Repeat with the rest of the mixture.

Bake for 15–20 minutes, or until the tops of the kibbab turn dark brown and they are cooked through.

Kibbab bi kishk
Kibbab ovals in kishk soup

serves 4–6

Citi has a pot of this soup simmering throughout winter. Whenever I taste it, it takes me back to her kitchen, sipping the soup while soaking up the warmth of the fire.

1 quantity uncooked kibbab ovals (see opposite page)
250 g (9 oz/1½ cups) ready-made kishk (see Note)
3 garlic cloves, crushed
⅛ teaspoon salt

Place 3.5 litres (122 fl oz/14 cups) of water and the kishk in a saucepan and stir until it dissolves. Place over high heat, stirring occasionally, and bring to the boil. Crush the garlic with salt, using a mortar and pestle, add to the kishk and stir. Bring to the boil, then reduce the heat and simmer for 10 minutes. Add the kibbab and boil for 10 minutes.

Note: Kishk is a dried, granular yoghurt that is available from Lebanese grocery stores.

Oros kibbeh

Helmets

makes 9–10

150 g (5½ oz/¾ cup) fine crushed
    wheat (burghul)
1 quantity raw kibbeh (see page 120)

Hashweh (filling)
1 tablespoon vegetable oil, plus extra,
    for brushing
2 onions, finely chopped
250 g (9 oz) minced (ground) topside
    beef or lamb
125 g (4 oz) butter
¼ teaspoon finely ground Lebanese
    black pepper
¼ teaspoon ground cumin
⅛ teaspoon chilli powder
⅛ teaspoon ground cinnamon
40 g (1½ oz/¼ cup) pine nuts, toasted
35 g (1¼ oz/¼ cup) crumbled feta
    cheese, optional

Preheat the oven to 200°C (400°F/Gas 6). Wash the crushed wheat then soak in water for about 15 minutes. Drain and squeeze it thoroughly. Knead with the raw kibbeh.

To make the hashweh, heat the oil in a saucepan over low heat and cook the onion for about 10 minutes, or until soft. Remove from the pan and set aside in a bowl. Increase the heat to high, add the meat and cook until the juices have evaporated. Reduce the heat to low. Add the butter, pepper and spices and mix for 5 minutes until the meat is well cooked. Add to the bowl with the onion. Add the pine nuts and set aside to cool. Gently mix in the feta, if using.

To shape the helmets, you will need a round bowl that is 9 cm (3½ inches) diameter and 4 cm (1½ inches) deep. Line the inside of it with plastic wrap, with some overhanging. Brush two baking trays with vegetable oil.

Line a work surface with a piece of plastic wrap. For the base of the helmet, pat a handful of the kibbeh into a 12 cm (4½ inch) round diameter and about 5 mm (¼ inch) thick. The base has to be wider than the bowl. Pile 2 tablespoons of hashweh in the centre of the base.

Dampen the plastic of your lined bowl with some water. Grab enough kibbeh and press it with your fingers to line the inside of the bowl. This is the helmet, which goes on top of the base. Turn the bowl upside down on top of the base. Press down on the bowl, then lift it off. Remove the plastic and excess kibbeh and pat down the edges with wet fingers. Hold the helmet in your hand and inspect to see that the edges are sealed. Reuse any trimmings. Place the helmet on and brush the top with oil as well. Repeat with the remaining raw kibbeh and filling.

Bake for 15–20 minutes, or until the top of the helmets are dark brown and cooked through.

Kibbab bi laben
Kibbab ovals in yoghurt soup

serves 8

250 g (9 oz/1¼ cups) fine crushed
  wheat (burghul)

500 g (1 lb 2 oz) lean beef or lamb

40 g (1½ oz) butter

6 garlic cloves, crushed

220 g (7¾ oz/1 cup) medium-grain rice

1 tablespoon dried mint

1 tablespoon salt

2 litres (70 fl oz/8 cups) plain yoghurt

2 eggs

1 teaspoon bicarbonate of soda

Marhan

3 mint leaves, roughly chopped

2 basil leaves, roughly chopped

½ brown onion, roughly chopped

½ long red chilli, seeded and chopped,
  or ¼ teaspoon chilli powder

½ teaspoon finely ground Lebanese
  black pepper

1¼ teaspoons ground cumin or kibbeh
  spice mix (see page 22)

1½ teaspoons salt

Hashweh (filling)

1 tablespoon vegetable oil

2 onions, finely chopped

250 g (9 oz) minced (ground) topside
  beef or lamb

125 g (4½ oz) butter

¼ teaspoon finely ground Lebanese
  black pepper

¼ teaspoon ground cumin

⅛ teaspoon chilli powder

⅛ teaspoon ground cinnamon

To make the hashweh, heat the oil in a saucepan over low heat and cook the onion for about 10 minutes, or until soft. Remove from the pan and set aside in a bowl. Increase the heat to high, add the meat and cook until the juices have evaporated. Reduce the heat to low. Add the butter, pepper and spices and mix for 5 minutes, or until the meat is well cooked. Add to the bowl with the onion. Cool, then refrigerate until chilled.

Fill a bowl with ice and water. Wash the wheat then soak in the iced water and leave in the freezer for 15 minutes. Mince (grind) the meat three times. Freeze for 5 minutes.

To make the kibbab, put the minced meat and 1 teaspoon of the iced water in a food processor. Process until the meat is soft, finely processed and almost silky. Reserve about ¾ cup of the meat and chill the rest in the freezer until needed.

To make the marhan, put the ¾ cup meat and the rest of the ingredients in a food processor. Blend until creamy. Drain the burghul, then squeeze it thoroughly. Add it to the marhan along with the meat from the freezer. Dip your hands in iced water, then knead the mixture thoroughly.

Wet your hands and grab a handful of raw kibbeh. Mould it into an oval shape to fit the palm of your hand. Wet your index finger and poke through one end of the oval. Make a hollow by working around the hole by pressing against the palm of your hand to create a thin wall. Place 1 tablespoon of the filling in the hole. Wet your hand and close the kibbab. Set aside. Repeat.

To make the soup, heat the butter in a small saucepan over low heat, add the garlic and cook for 3 minutes. Boil 5.25 litres (184 fl oz/21 cups) of water in a large saucepan. Add the buttery garlic, rice, mint and salt. Boil for 5 minutes. Add the kibbab one at a time and boil for 10 minutes, stirring occasionally. Put the yoghurt, egg and bicarbonate of soda in a large bowl and mix using electric beaters for 3 minutes. Slowly add to the boiling water, stirring until it returns to the boil, then boil for a further 7 minutes. Turn off the heat and rest, uncovered, for a few minutes before serving.

130

Kibbeh bi sayneeh
Baked kibbeh

serves 6–8

Hashweh (filling)

1 tablespoon vegetable oil

2 onions, finely chopped

250 g (9 oz) minced (ground) topside
 beef or lamb

125 g (4 oz) butter

¼ teaspoon finely ground Lebanese
 black pepper

¼ teaspoon ground cumin

⅛ teaspoon chilli powder

⅛ teaspoon ground cinnamon

40 g (1½ oz/¼ cup) pine nuts, toasted

250 g (9 oz/1⅔ cups) crumbled feta
 cheese, optional

500 g (1 lb 2 oz/2½ cups) fine crushed
 wheat (burghul)

1 kg (2 lb 4 oz) lean beef or lamb
 chunks

vegetable oil, for greasing and to cover

Marhan

5 mint leaves, roughly chopped

4 basil leaves, roughly chopped

1 brown onion, roughly chopped

1 long red chilli, seeded and chopped,
 or ¼ teaspoon chilli powder

1 teaspoon finely ground Lebanese
 black pepper

2½ teaspoons ground cumin or kibbeh
 spice mix (see page 22)

3 teaspoons salt

To make the hashweh, heat the oil in a saucepan over low heat and cook the onion for about 10 minutes, or until soft. Remove from the pan and set aside in a bowl. Increase the heat to high, add the meat and cook until the juices have evaporated. Reduce the heat to low. Add the butter, pepper and spices and mix for 5 minutes until the meat is well cooked. Add to the bowl with the onion. Add the pine nuts and mix thoroughly. Set aside to cool and refrigerate until chilled.

Preheat the oven to 200°C (400°F/Gas 6). Fill a bowl with ice cubes and water. Wash the crushed wheat then soak in the iced water and leave in the freezer for about 15 minutes. Mince (grind) the meat three times (or ask your butcher to do this for you). Put the meat in the freezer for 5 minutes.

To make the kibbeh, put the minced meat and 1 teaspoon of iced water in a food processor. Process until the meat is soft, finely processed and almost silky. Reserve about ¾ cup of the meat and chill the rest in the freezer until needed.

To make the marhan, put the ¾ cup meat and the rest of the ingredients in a food processor. Blend until creamy. Drain the burghul, then squeeze it thoroughly. Add it to the marhan along with the meat from the freezer. Dip your hands in iced water, then knead the mixture thoroughly.

Grease the bottom of a 33 cm (13 inch) round cake tin with oil. Dampen your hands in some water and place half of the kibbeh to cover the base of the prepared tin, smoothing the top. Fill the middle layer with the hashweh combined with feta, if using. Cover with the rest of the kibbeh. With a wet knife, score the top into even diagonal pieces. Using your finger, poke a hole through the layers in the dish. Cover the top with a thin layer of vegetable oil so that it trickles into the hole. Place in the oven and watch carefully. When the oil begins to sizzle, set the timer for 20 minutes and bake until golden and cooked.

Shish kebab

makes 14

Shish kebabs are made even tastier when dipped into hummous, babba ganoush or garlic sauce. For me, they are a taste of summer.

1 kg (2 lb 4 oz) lamb shoulder, diced
    into pieces about 3 cm (1¼ inch)
salt
350 g (12 oz) cherry tomatoes or
    4 tomatoes, cut into chunky cubes
3 onions, cut into chunky cubes
500 g (1 lb 2 oz) button mushrooms
2 red or green capsicums (peppers),
    cut into chunky pieces

Soak 14 wooden skewers for 30 minutes before use.

Season the meat with salt. Thread the meat and vegetables onto the skewers, alternating every two pieces of meat with a few pieces of the vegetables. Leave about 1 cm (½ inch) from the top of the skewer and about 4 cm (1½ inches) from the bottom free.

Preheat a barbecue grill to medium heat and cook the kebabs for 4–5 minutes each side, turning once, until cooked to your liking. Alternatively, you can cook them under a grill (broiler) for the same time.

Shish tawook
Marinated chicken

serves 8

Shish tawook makes my mouth water right from the beginning when I am making it. The marinated chicken can be rolled into Lebanese bread and made into sandwiches. We like to wrap it with hummous, pickled turnip, pickled cucumber and some salad leaves.

4 garlic cloves, crushed
1 teaspoon salt
4 tablespoons olive oil
juice of 1 lemon
2 tablespoons white vinegar
1 tablespoon dried oregano
1 kg (2 lb 4 oz) chicken breast fillets, cut in half horizontally

In a large bowl, combine the garlic, salt, oil, lemon, vinegar and oregano. Mix well until well blended.

Add the chicken to the marinade and mix through. Leave to marinate overnight in the fridge.

Preheat a barbecue grill to medium heat and cook the chicken for 2–3 minutes each side or until cooked through. Alternatively, you can cook the chicken in a frying pan over medium heat for the same amount of time.

Notes: You can cut the chicken into 3 cm (1¼ inch) pieces and thread onto skewers, if you prefer. If you do this, omit the oregano from the marinade.

Chicken thigh fillets also work well for this recipe.

Shawarama

Kebab rolls

makes 6

1 kg (2 lb 4 oz) lamb backstraps
   or loin fillet
1 tablespoon olive oil
6 pieces Lebanese bread
½ iceberg lettuce, shredded
3 tomatoes, sliced
1 red onion, sliced
1 handful flat-leaf (Italian) parsley,
   chopped
Hummous (see page 38), babba
   ghanoush (see page 39) or garlic
   sauce (see page 42), to serve

Marinade
2 garlic cloves, crushed
1 tablespoon olive oil
1 tablespoon white vinegar
250 ml (9 fl oz/1 cup) red wine
1 teaspoon my family's baharat
   spice mix (see page 22)
¼ teaspoon chilli powder
¼ teaspoon salt

For the marinade, place all the ingredients in a bowl. Add the meat and marinate for at least 2 hours. Aunty Rosa likes to marinate the meat overnight for a stronger flavour.

Preheat a large frying pan over medium–high heat, add the oil and cook the meat, turning once, until cooked to your liking.

To make the rolls, lay out the Lebanese bread and top each one with some lettuce, tomato, onion, parsley, lamb and your choice of topping. Roll up tightly to serve.

Rooz a deejesh
Boiled rice cooked in chicken stock

serves 4–6

This is my Mum, Joumana's, speciality.

60 g (2¼ oz) butter

2 onions, quartered

1 kg (2 lb 4 oz) chicken thigh fillets

1 cinnamon stick

440 g (15½ oz/2 cups) medium-grain rice, washed very well

1 teaspoon salt

⅛ teaspoon ground cinnamon

115 g (4 oz/¾ cup) pine nuts

40 g (1½ oz/⅓ cup) slivered almonds

Heat 20 g (¾ oz) of the butter in a saucepan over medium heat and cook the onion until soft. Add the chicken and cinnamon stick and cook, stirring, for about 20 minutes, or until browned and cooked through. Pour 2 litres (70 fl oz/8 cups) of boiling water into the pan. Bring to the boil and simmer for 30 minutes. Pour the mixture into a strainer with a bowl underneath to capture the stock.

Melt the remaining butter in a saucepan over low heat. Mix in the rice, salt and cinnamon. Pour 1 litre (35 fl oz/4 cups) of the chicken stock into the pan. Bring to the boil. Reduce the heat, cover with a lid and simmer for 10–15 minutes, or until the rice is cooked.

Separately toast the pine nuts and slivered almonds in a non-stick frying pan until golden brown.

Once the chicken has cooled down, use your hands to break it into chunky pieces, then set aside. Discard the onion wedges.

This dish is usually presented on a large oval platter. The rice is mounded on the platter, then smoothed out. The chicken pieces are placed on top of the rice, then the almonds and pine nuts are sprinkled over the top.

◆ Lessons in Hospitality

Usbeh maqlii
Pan-fried liver

serves 4

Lamb or calf liver can be cooked, as here, or even eaten raw as long as it is ultra fresh. Cut small pieces and serve with a small plate that has 1 teaspoon salt, 1 teaspoon chill powder and 1 teaspoon finely ground Lebanese black pepper mixed together. Dip the pieces into the seasoning and eat—alternatively, you can wrap the pieces in Lebanese bread.

500 g (1 lb 2 oz) lamb or calf liver
⅛ teaspoon my family's baharat spice mix (see page 22)
⅛ teaspoon chilli powder
⅛ teaspoon salt
1 tablespoon olive oil
juice of ½ lemon

Peel the membrane off the liver. If buying the liver as a whole, cut strips that are about 6 cm (2½ inches) long and about 5 mm (¼ inch) thick. Cut off any fatty pieces and veins so that you are left with a clean surface.

Season the liver with the baharat, chilli and salt. Heat a non-stick frying pan over high heat, add the oil and cook the liver until it changes to a light–medium brown colour or until cooked to your liking.

Remove from the heat and drizzle with lemon juice.

Alb maqlii
Pan-fried heart strips

serves 4

Cook heart the same as you would liver or kidney but the slices have to be much thinner.

500 g (1 lb 2 oz) lamb or calf heart
⅛ teaspoon my family's baharat spice mix (see page 22)
⅛ teaspoon chilli powder
⅛ teaspoon salt
1 tablespoon olive oil
juice of ½ lemon

Peel the membrane off the heart. Slice the heart into thin strips and season with the baharat, chilli powder and salt. Heat the oil in a non-stick frying pan over high heat and cook the heart strips until they change to a brown colour, or until cooked to your liking.

Remove from the heat and drizzle with lemon juice. Serve with plenty of salad to freshen the palate.

Al-saman ibtabel

Marinated quail

serves 6

6 quails
3 garlic cloves
½ teaspoon salt, plus extra
juice of 1 lemon or 3 tablespoons
    white vinegar
3 tablespoons olive oil
2 teaspoons dried oregano

Wash the quails and place in a colander to drain. Remove the backbones, open the quails out and flatten them slightly.

Rub the quails with the salt. Crush the garlic with the salt using a mortar and pestle. Transfer the crushed garlic to a large non-metallic bowl. Add the lemon or vinegar, oil and oregano to the garlic. Place the quails in the marinade for 2–24 hours.

Preheat a barbecue grill to medium heat and cook the quails for 5 minutes each side or until cooked to your liking.

Salatat lisaanat

Tongue salad

serves 8

12 lambs' tongues or 1 beef tongue
1 cinnamon stick
¼ teaspoon salt
3 garlic cloves
1 tablespoon lemon juice
1 tablespoon olive oil
2 tablespoons fresh mint, finely
    chopped, or 1 tablespoon dried mint
1 handful flat-leaf (Italian) parsley,
    finely chopped
½ teaspoon chilli powder, optional

Place the tongues or tongue and cinnamon stick in a saucepan with enough water to cover, bring to the boil, season with some salt and simmer for 1½ hours for lamb or 2 hours for beef, or until tender and cooked. Transfer to a strainer and leave until cool enough to touch. Peel the skin off with your hands. Dice the tongue and set aside.

Crush the garlic with the salt. Put in a large bowl, add the lemon juice, oil and diced tongue and toss together. Sprinkle in the mint, parsley and chilli powder, if using.

Note: Tongue can be eaten plain after it is boiled and peeled; this is ideal with garlic sauce (see page 42).

Kilya maqlii
Pan-fried kidney
serves 4

Cooking kidneys is very similar to cooking liver, but takes a little bit longer.

500 g (1 lb 2 oz) lamb or calf kidney
⅛ teaspoon my family's baharat spice
   mix (see page 22)
⅛ teaspoon chilli powder
⅛ teaspoon salt
1 tablespoon olive oil
juice of ½ lemon

Peel the membrane off the kidney. Slice the kidney into strips and season with the baharat, chilli and salt. Heat the oil in a non-stick frying pan over high heat and cook the kidney to a light or medium brown colour or until cooked to your liking.

Remove from the heat and drizzle with lemon juice.

Gummeh
Stuffed tripe

serves 6–8

2 kg (4 lb 8 oz) lamb or beef tripe
75 g (2¾ oz/½ cup) plain
(all-purpose) flour
1 tablespoon salt
2 lemons, cut into wedges
125 ml (4 fl oz/½ cup) white vinegar

Stuffing
155 g (5½ oz/1 cup) pine nuts
185 g (6½ oz) butter
750 g (1 lb 10 oz) minced (ground)
lamb
165 g (5¾ oz/¾ cup) medium-grain
rice, washed and drained
4 onions, chopped
1¼ teaspoons my family's baharat
spice mix (see page 22)

Turn the tripe inside out and put in a large sink with the flour, salt, lemon and vinegar. Mix to coat the tripe. Soak for 30 minutes, then scrub it with your hands as if hand washing clothes. Rinse thoroughly. Cut into 10 cm (4 inch) squares.

Turn the tripe right-side out, so that the rough-textured part is on the outside, then place the tripe pieces in a strainer over a bowl. Use a needle and thread to sew the pockets into a 10 cm x 5 cm (4 inch x 2 inch) rectangle, leaving one of the short sides open for the stuffing.

For the stuffing, toast the pine nuts in a frying pan until golden. Remove from the pan. Melt the butter in the pan, add the lamb and cook for about 10 minutes, or until the meat begins to brown. Set aside to cool, then mix with the pine nuts, rice, onion and baharat.

Fill the tripe pockets three-quarters full with the stuffing and seal the opening by sewing with cotton.

Place the tripe in a large saucepan and cover with 5 litres (20 cups/175 fl oz) of water. Bring to the boil over high heat and scoop off the scum that rises to the surface. Reduce the heat and simmer for 1½–2 hours. It's ready when the tripe is soft and tender. Pull the cotton out and eat.

Note: You can use a normal needle and cotton thread to sew the tripe pockets.

4
The Family
Cleansing
the Spirit

Fasting to Feasting

'Throughout the years the food has remained the same, the family togetherness has remained the same.'

Aunty Rosa

Throughout the year, our Maronite Catholic calendar marks religious events that are celebrated through rituals and family gatherings. The most widely recognised in our family are the rituals of fasting and abstinence that are practised in the days leading up to Easter and Christmas. The Great Fast, otherwise known as the 40-day fast of Lent, is performed in the lead up to Easter. It's a chance to reflect on the forty days that Jesus spent in the desert before he was crucified. The Little Fast is carried out nine days before Christmas and is symbolic of the nine months that Mary was pregnant with Jesus. The idea of fasting is to go without food from midnight until midday.

Lent

An assortment of favourite vegetarian and fish dishes that are usually overshadowed by the meaty ones are revisited and enjoyed during the time of Lent. The devout, including my mother, give up meat, dairy, sweets and coffee. Mum displays her strength by giving up her favourite indulgences such as cheese, bread and coffee. 'It's all in the mind,' she says. This woman who 'can't function without coffee' sets her mind, body and spirit into motion. As of the first day of Lent, Ash Monday, she transforms her diet and relishes in being closer to her faith. She also takes this time to reflect on her personal relationships and tries to make amends where needed. By the end of it she admits, 'my body feels wonderful'. Then she carefully reintroduces her favourites back into her diet. 'Coffee and cheese are usually top of my list,' she explains.

Citi Leila was always impressed to see her grandchildren practising the rituals of Lent. One year I decided that I would join her and my mother in giving up meat for Lent. On one particular day in the middle of Lent, I headed to Citi's house after school. It was around midday and I had just finished an exam. Feeling famished, my nose and appetite could not help being seduced by the smell of Citi's chicken and tomato soup—the soup she made when we were sick. She was cooking the batch for Gidi, who was not well at the time. Unable to control the hunger pangs, I couldn't wait for Citi to get off the phone, so I helped myself to a serving. When she returned to the kitchen, she found me sitting and enjoying a bowl of soup. 'My sweetheart,' she said, 'I thought you were giving up meat for Lent?' Confused, I responded, 'I am! That's why I'm removing the chicken pieces.' At this she burst into laughter and, until this day, no Lent has gone by without Citi re-telling that story. Secretly I think it helps her get through it.

Easter and Christmas

When my siblings and I were small and manageable, Mum would have us sporting our finest clothes to look our best for the early-morning church services every Sunday. St. Maroun's in Redfern was the family favourite for many years. It's where a tight community of Lebanese that had emigrated from Becharee met every week. After each service, they would congregate outside the church and talk for hours. Come Easter and Christmas, everybody made an effort to wear their finery; it was like the Oscars had come

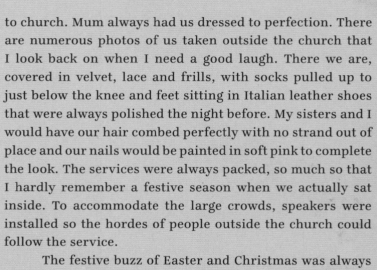

to church. Mum always had us dressed to perfection. There are numerous photos of us taken outside the church that I look back on when I need a good laugh. There we are, covered in velvet, lace and frills, with socks pulled up to just below the knee and feet sitting in Italian leather shoes that were always polished the night before. My sisters and I would have our hair combed perfectly with no strand out of place and our nails would be painted in soft pink to complete the look. The services were always packed, so much so that I hardly remember a festive season when we actually sat inside. To accommodate the large crowds, speakers were installed so the hordes of people outside the church could follow the service.

The festive buzz of Easter and Christmas was always heightened the moment we entered Citi's house. Aunty Rosa captures the feeling perfectly: 'Driving to Mum's house, the journey always felt too long. There was this anticipation and excitement; we couldn't wait to see each other.' Christmas and Easter have always been held at Citi's house. With more than forty-five of us, including her children and their families, there is hardly a dull or quiet moment when we get together. From the moment we all begin to arrive at the house we can't help ourselves from hugging, cheek pinching and kissing each other. Once the explosive energy of greeting each other settles, the controlled chaos of the preparations begins. 'When we all get together and cook, you can't describe it,' says Aunty Hind. 'It's sheer enjoyment and a feeling of togetherness; we always get so excited to be in each other's company.'

My favourite childhood memories are the ones at Citi's house during these festive celebrations. Here is a brief snapshot of how the day unfolds...

Tantalising smells emanate from Citi's kitchen and her back-up kitchen (the laundry). Having been to midnight mass the night before, Citi is up at the crack of dawn. She likes to cook her specialty dishes such as tripe and kibbeh in her back-up kitchen. The main kitchen is left for others.

Bunches of washed parsley lie on a cotton sheet spread on the kitchen table; a box of juicy red tomatoes sits underneath. They await the talented hands of Aunty Rosa to chop them for the tabbouleh. She will call on the many nieces and nephews to help with juicing the lemons and chopping the onions. Standing directly opposite is Aunty Hind, who is on hummous duty. My Mum is usually in the middle of it all. She likes to keep a kitchen towel thrown over one of her shoulders as she juggles a few dishes on the stove and in the oven. Before the dishes are placed on the table under the long pergola in the backyard, Aunty Therese gives them some final touches. Presentation has always been just as important as the taste of the dish itself. 'I always decorate the platters and give them the final touches,' she explains. In the backyard, the men sit around the barbecue taking turns cooking the meat. The grandchildren are trying to set the table perfectly. Each year the task of trying to fit the food along one table gets harder as the family grows. Those who don't make it onto the main table spread themselves throughout the yard and house.

Underneath the two-metre-high faux Christmas tree in the formal lounge lay the presents. A few weeks before Christmas, names are drawn and each person is responsible for buying a small token present for another. The presents are opened after the meal and the room is transformed into a paper-tearing, ribbon-flying blizzard. Shrieks of laughter and excitement echo through the house for hours.

Kibbet il roheb
Monk's kibbeh soup (Good Friday soup)

serves about 8

150 g (5½ oz/¾ cup) dried borlotti
    beans
150 g (5½ oz/¾ cup) dried chickpeas
    (garbanzos)
4 tablespoons olive oil
3 brown onions
500 g (1 lb 2 oz) silverbeet (Swiss
    chard), shredded
lemon juice, to serve

Balls
265 g (9½ oz/1½ cups) fine crushed
    wheat (burghul)
2 onions, finely chopped
salt
1 teaspoon ground cumin
1 teaspoon finely ground Lebanese
    black pepper
¼ pumpkin (winter squash), steamed
    or boiled and mashed
1 tablespoon fresh mint leaves,
    chopped, or 1 teaspoon dried mint
⅛ teaspoon chilli powder, optional
110 g (3¾ oz/¾ cup) plain
    (all-purpose) flour, plus extra

Soak the borlotti beans and chickpeas separately overnight.
Rinse and drain.

Meanwhile, soak the burghul for the balls in 500 ml
(17 fl oz/2 cups) of warm water for 30 minutes. Drain and
squeeze to remove excess water.

Place the beans and chickpeas in a saucepan with 3 litres
(105 fl oz/12 cups) of water. Cook over medium heat for about
1 hour, or until they just begin to soften. Reduce the heat to low
and add 250 ml (9 fl oz/1 cup) of water to settle the water. Keep
over low heat.

Heat the oil in a frying pan over low heat and cook the onion
until golden and translucent. Add to the beans and chickpeas.
Stir, partially cover with the lid and keep over low heat.

Meanwhile, for the balls, rub the onion with some salt
and transfer to a large bowl. Add the rest of the ingredients,
including the crushed wheat. Scrunch the mixture with your
hands and knead to get an even consistency.

Roll 2 teaspoons of the mixture between your palms into a
sausage shape, then roll into a 2.5 cm (1 inch) ball. The ball
should feel nice and firm—if it feels soft, add a little more flour
to the mixture. Repeat with the remaining mixture.

Bring the soup mixture to the boil, then add the balls, one at
a time, to the boiling water and beans. Stir occasionally to stop
the balls from clinging to each other. Add the silverbeet, stir
gently and cook for about 10–15 minutes.

Drizzle lemon juice into the soup just before serving.

Note: The burghul mixture can also be moulded into patties,
brushed with oil and pan-fried.

Kibbeh otah
Vegetarian kibbeh ovals

Makes 20

vegetable oil, for brushing

500 g (1 lb 2 oz) crushed wheat (burghul)

⅛ pumpkin (winter squash), cooked and mashed

1 onion, finely grated

1 tablespoon fresh mint leaves, chopped or 1 teaspoon dried mint

about 150 g (5½ oz/1 cup) plain (all-purpose) flour

¼ teaspoon finely ground Lebanese black pepper

1 teaspoon ground cumin

1½ teaspoons sea salt

Filling

220 g (7¾ oz/1 cup) dried split chickpeas (garbanzos) (available from a Lebanese grocer)

2 teaspoons olive oil

2 onions, chopped

½ bunch silverbeet (Swiss chard), leaves shredded

⅛ teaspoon ground cumin

⅛ teaspoon chilli powder

⅛ teaspoon finely ground Lebanese black pepper

⅛ teaspoon salt

For the filling, soak the chickpeas in water overnight. Rinse and drain.

Place the chickpeas in a saucepan of water and bring to the boil. Boil for 20 minutes. Remove from the heat, then drain.

Heat the oil in a saucepan over low heat and cook the onion until soft and translucent. Add the chickpeas and stir for about 10 minutes. Add the silverbeet, spices and seasoning and stir occasionally for 5 minutes. Remove from the heat and place in a bowl. Allow to cool.

Preheat the oven to 200°C (400°F/Gas 6). Brush a baking tray with oil.

For the kibbeh, soak the burghul in 500 ml (17 fl oz/2 cups) of warm water for 30 minutes. Strain the burghul in a sieve, then squeeze it in your hands to remove as much water as possible. Add the burghul to a large bowl along with the rest of the ingredients. Mix together.

Dampen your hands with some water and grab a handful of vegetarian kibbeh. Mould into an oval shape to fit the palm of your hand. Wet your index finger and poke through one end of the oval. Make a hollow by working around the hole by pressing against the palm of your hand to create a thin wall. Place 1 tablespoon of the filling into the hollowed opening. Wet your hand and gently close the oval. Place the oval on the tray, then brush the top with oil. Repeat with the rest of the mixture.

Bake for 15–20 minutes or until golden. Alternatively, deep-fry them in oil heated to 180°C (350°F) and cook for no more than 5 minutes, or until lightly golden.

Note: You can use these stuffed vegetarian kibbeh ovals in the Monk's kibbeh soup (see page 156) instead of the balls. Add the cooked ovals to the soup just before serving. You can also use this dough to make patties. Mould the mixture into patties, brush with oil and pan-fry them until golden.

Olab hoodrah

Vegetable stack

serves 6–8

220 g (7¾ oz/1 cup) dried split
  chickpeas (garbanzos) (available
  from a Lebanese grocer)
2 large eggplants (aubergines),
  peeled and cut into 1 cm (½ inch)
  thick slices
vegetable oil, for brushing
1 teaspoon salt
1 teaspoon ground cumin
4 onions, sliced into rings
500 g (1 lb 2 oz) button mushrooms,
  sliced
1 red capsicum (pepper), sliced
  into rings
1 green capsicum (pepper), sliced
  into rings
4 tomatoes, sliced into rounds
1 tablespoon tomato paste
  (concentrated purée)

Soak the split chickpeas in water overnight. Rinse and drain.

Brush the eggplant with some oil. In a frying pan over high heat, sear the eggplant in batches on both sides.

Combine the salt and cumin. In a large saucepan create layers starting with the onion, then the chickpeas, eggplant, mushroom and capsicum, sprinkling with the salt–cumin mixture as you go. Add the tomato as the final layer.

Dissolve the tomato paste in 250 ml (9 fl oz/1 cup) of water and pour over the vegetables. Bring to the boil, cover with a lid and simmer for 30–40 minutes, or until the vegetables are cooked and tender.

Note: Serve with mashed potato or Boiled rice with egg noodles (see page 36).

Marshoosheh
Cabbage with coarse crushed wheat

serves 4

'The more onions the tastier.' My mother, Joumana

3 tablespoons olive oil
2 brown onions, finely chopped
1 long red chilli, seeded and chopped
½ head small green cabbage, shredded
   or finely chopped
90 g (3¼ oz/½ cup) coarse crushed
   wheat (burghul)
salt

Heat the oil in a saucepan over medium heat. Add the onion and chilli. Cook the onion until it begins to turn golden. Add the cabbage and crushed wheat and mix. Reduce the heat, cover with a lid and simmer for 15 minutes. Season with salt and serve.

Arnabiit maqlii
Fried cauliflower

serves 4–6

1 cauliflower
vegetable oil, for deep-frying
150 g (5½ oz/1 cup) plain (all-purpose)
   flour
3 eggs

Wash the cauliflower and separate the florets. Steam until they begin to soften. They have to be slightly soft but firm. Set aside until cool enough to handle, then cut in half.

Heat the oil in a large saucepan to 160°C (315°F). Spread the flour out on a plate. In a bowl whisk the eggs. Coat the cauliflower with flour, then dip in the egg. Make sure the cauliflower is soaked with the egg. Fry a few florets at a time until golden brown. Drain the cauliflower on a wire rack.

M'Juderah

Lentils and rice

serves 6–8

400 g (14 oz/2 cups) brown lentils

4 tablespoons olive oil

3 onions, chopped

100 g (3½ oz) long-grain or medium-grain brown or white rice

2 teaspoons salt

Wash the lentils thoroughly and rummage through to see if there are any stones.

In a saucepan, heat the oil over medium heat and cook the onion until golden brown (this will make the dish flavoursome). Add the lentils and stir to combine. If you are using brown rice add it at the same time as the lentils.

Add 2 litres (70 fl oz/8 cups) of water and the salt, cover with a lid and bring to the boil over high heat. Boil the lentils for 30 minutes, or until they begin to soften. If the lentils look dry, add more water. If you are using white rice, add it now and bring to the boil again. Reduce the heat and simmer for up to 10 minutes, or until the rice and lentils are cooked.

Scoop the mixture into a casserole dish straight away—it should be slightly runny. Allow to rest, uncovered, for about 20 minutes—the lentils and rice will soak up the extra moisture and slightly dry up.

It can be served right away or eaten cold. It is delicious with a dollop of laben (see page 30) or labneh (see page 31).

Note: A cold serving of lentils and rice goes well with the Tomato and dried mint salad (see page 63) and also the Green cabbage salad (see page 54).

Falafel

Makes 28

In this recipe you have the option to use a falafel instrument or mould the falafel with your hands. A falafel instrument is similar to an ice-cream scoop. Falafel can be eaten as part of a banquet type spread of pickles, salad greens and vegetables, tahini sauce, garlic sauce and babba ghanoush.

250 g (9 oz/1½ cups) dried broad (fava) beans (whole or split)

100 g (3½ oz/½ cup) dried chickpeas (garbanzos)

1 small handful coriander (cilantro), chopped

2 tablespoons chopped mint

1 onion, roughly chopped

5 garlic cloves

1 small bunch flat-leaf (Italian) parsley, chopped

1 teaspoon salt

1 teaspoon falafel spice mix

1 long red or green chilli, seeded and chopped, optional

vegetable oil, for deep-frying

Combine the broad beans and chickpeas in a large bowl. Soak in water overnight. Rinse and drain.

Place all the ingredients except the oil in a bowl and toss to mix. Add 1 cup of the mixture at a time to a food processor, then pulse until the mixture becomes a green soft paste. You can test if it is ready by grabbing some of the mixture; if you can mould it and it holds together well, then it is ready.

Heat some oil in a narrow saucepan to 180°C (350°F/Gas 4).

If you are using your hands, make flat rounds that are 2 cm (¾ inch) thick and about 5.5 cm (2¼ inch) in diameter. Drop a few at a time into the hot oil and deep-fry the balls in batches until golden on one side, then turn over and cook the other side. Drain on paper towel and serve.

If you are using a falafel instrument, mould the mixture onto it with a spoon and release the balls into the hot oil and cook in the same way.

Note: To make a Falafel roll, split a piece of Lebanese bread in half around the seams and lay the pieces on top of each other— this will make a tighter roll. Cut a few falafel in half and place in the middle of the bread. Add some chopped lettuce, sliced tomato, sliced onion and sliced pickles. Drizzle tahini sauce on top. Roll the bread up tightly.

Hindbeh maslooa ma'a basal
Blanched endives with onion

serves 4

1 bunch curly endive
1 tablespoon vegetable oil
4 onions, cut into thin wedges
1 teaspoon olive oil
juice of ½ lemon
salt

Wash the endive and discard the bottom stems. Cut the bunch of leaves into three or four chunks.

Cook the endive in boiling salted water for up to 30 minutes or until very tender. The endive will change colour from light green to dark green. Transfer to a colander and allow to cool. Squeeze out any remaining water.

Heat the oil in a frying pan over medium heat and cook the onion until golden and soft. Transfer to a plate and set aside.

Heat the olive oil the same pan and lightly toss the endive for about 1 minute. Remove from the heat and mix in the lemon juice and season with salt.

Transfer to a platter. Scatter the onion on top to serve.

Kibbet batata
Potato and parsley mince
serves 4–6

5 potatoes
1 handful flat-leaf (Italian) parsley,
  roughly chopped
5 mint leaves, finely chopped
1 red chilli, chopped, optional
½ teaspoon salt
olive oil, to serve
chilli powder, to serve

Peel and wash the potatoes and cut into chunks. Boil them until they are soft. Remove from the heat, then strain and allow to cool.

Combine the potato, herbs, chilli and salt in a food processor and blend until a creamy consistency.

To serve, drizzle the mince with olive oil and sprinkle with chilli powder.

Note: We usually eat this with Lebanese bread, or just on its own. It's also delicious with lots of green leaves and vegetables.

Amheeyeah with laben
Barley with yoghurt
serves 6

This dish is traditionally served chilled.

440 g (15½ oz/2 cups) barley
2 garlic cloves, optional
1 teaspoon salt
1 litre (35 fl oz/4 cups) plain yoghurt
  or laben (see page 30)
1 tablespoon dried mint

Put the barley and 2 litres (70 fl oz/8 cups) of water in a saucepan and bring to the boil over high heat. Reduce the heat and simmer for up to 1½ hours, or until the barley is tender.

Remove the barley from the heat, drain well and set aside to cool completely.

Crush the garlic, if using, with the salt using a mortar and pestle. Place the yoghurt in a bowl and mix in the garlic and the dried mint. Add the barley and mix well. Serve chilled.

Good Friday

My memories of Good Friday always include images of my mum getting up early in the morning to make her special soup, Kibbet il Roheb or Monk's Kibbeh Soup (see page 156). As she chopped, diced and stirred, she played her angelic Maronite Catholic CDs and sang along beautifully. It's amazing that she still has such a strong voice considering she lost a percentage of it due to surgery. She injured her vocal chords as a result of years of using her voice as an instrument of discipline for her five children— I can still hear the echo of her admonishments ringing through my ears from time to time.

The soup is made early in the day in order to be consumed after attending mid-morning Mass on Good Friday. When we were children it was supposed to be our consolation prize for fasting until midday and lasting through an overcrowded and longer than usual church service.

Each year I look forward to the advent of Good Friday so that my mother can make this once-a-year, mouth-watering delight. I love to individually pick out and eat the little flavoursome burghul balls swimming in the rich thick soup of borlotti beans and chickpeas. Slowly and carefully I sink my teeth through the burghul, pumpkin and mint balls, savouring every second.

The holy soup created a division between my siblings when we were growing up. On one side there were those of us who didn't mind sipping

on the soup all day long. But sometimes my younger sisters and brothers threatened to eat meat instead on this strictly no-meat-eating Catholic day. Citi Leila would usually spend Good Friday at our house to have a break from the festive preparations at her own house. One year she decided that she had enough of the divisions between the siblings and the threats to eat meat, so she embarked on the mission of reinventing the way we ate this dish. Staying faithful to the sacred ingredients of Monk's Kibbeh Soup, she scrapped the soup and came up with vegetarian patties and vegetarian kibbeh ovals (see page 161) instead. It was very clever and she borrowed the techniques used to make the original meat versions made from kibbeh. The patties and the

shells of the stuffed ovals are made in the same way that the balls for the soup are made. They are just shaped and cooked differently. We fry them or bake them in the oven. The shells are stuffed with split chickpeas, onions and spinach and seasoned with herbs and spices.

Since Citi's reinvention of the classic soup, no meat-eating threats have been made on Good Friday at our house. My favourite soup has been transformed in such a way that these days it has us all eating it in one way or another, whether as the traditional soup or as vegetarian patties, which are dipped into labneh, hummous and babba ghanoush, served as part of a banquet with leafy greens from the garden and a selection of piquant pickles.

Samak maglii
Fried fish

serves 4

4 fillets or 4 small whole fish (snapper or silver bream), cleaned and scaled
salt
plain (all-purpose) flour, for coating
vegetable oil, for shallow-frying

Sprinkle the fish with a little salt about 30 minutes before cooking and place in a colander.

Remove the fish from the colander and coat in seasoned flour. Shallow-fry the fish in batches until golden and just cooked through; the flesh should flake when tested with a fork.

Samak al salmon ma'a khoodrah
Pan-fried salmon with vegetables

serves 4

2 tablespoons olive oil
4 garlic cloves, finely chopped
1 green capsicum (pepper), finely chopped
1 red capsicum (pepper), finely chopped
4 soft cooking tomatoes, diced
1 small red chilli, chopped
salt
4 salmon cutlets
1 tablespoon finely chopped coriander (cilantro)

Heat half of the oil in a frying pan over medium heat and add the garlic, capsicum, tomato and chilli. Cook for a few minutes, or until they begin to soften. Season with some salt.

In a separate large non-stick frying pan, heat the remaining oil over high heat and sear the salmon cutlets on one side. Reduce the heat, turn the salmon over and spoon the capsicum–tomato salsa on top. Sprinkle with the coriander, cover and cook for up to 10 minutes or until cooked through and the fish flakes when tested with a fork.

Siadeeyeah
Rice cooked in fish stock

serves 4

Mum came up with this recipe during Lent. I think it was to compensate for us missing her famous chicken and rice dish. The chunky fish pieces and rice make it a satisfying and filling meal.

1 kg (2 lb 4 oz) whole snapper, cleaned
   and scaled
2 tablespoons olive oil, plus extra,
   for brushing
salt
1 lemon, cut into small thin wedges
440 g (15½ oz/2 cups) medium-grain
   rice
¼ teaspoon ground cinnamon
155 g (5½ oz/1 cup) pine nuts
40 g (1½ oz/¼ cup) blanched almonds,
   halved

Stock

2 teaspoons olive oil
1 onion, quartered
500 g (1 lb 2 oz) snapper heads and
   bones
1 cinnamon stick
1 bay leaf
1 teaspoon salt

To make the stock, heat the oil in a saucepan over medium heat and cook the onion until soft and translucent. Add the fish heads and bones, cinnamon stick, bay leaf, salt and 1.5 litres (52 fl oz/6 cups) of hot water. Bring to the boil, reduce the heat and simmer, covered, for 40 minutes. Tip the stock into a sieve over a bowl. Squeeze out as much liquid as possible from the fish heads and bones, then discard the solids.

Preheat the oven to 150°C (300°F/Gas 2). Line a baking tray with a large sheet of foil. Brush the snapper with some oil and place on the tray. Sprinkle the fish with some salt and place the lemon wedges inside and on top of the fish. Wrap the fish in foil and bake for 23–30 minutes, or until the flesh flakes when tested with a fork. Remove from the heat and allow to cool enough to handle. Remove the meaty flesh from the bones. Discard everything except for the flesh of the fish.

Heat 2 tablespoons of oil in a saucepan over low heat, add the rice and ground cinnamon. Add 1 litre (35 fl oz/4 cups) of stock and bring to the boil, then reduce the heat, cover with a lid and simmer for 15 minutes.

Meanwhile, separately toast the pine nuts and almonds in a frying pan until they are lightly golden.

This dish is usually presented on a large oval platter. Make a mound of rice on the platter, then smooth it out. Place the fish on top, then sprinkle with the nuts.

Sumkeh harra
Chilli fish
serves 4–6

Citi loves to cook this on her cast-iron wood-burning stove in the winter. The fire is usually burning all through the winter time. She uses it to keep warm and cook most of her dishes. You can use one large or two smaller whole fish, such as silver bream, snapper or red snapper which have been cleaned and scaled. Another option is to use fish fillets.

2 kg (4 lb 8 oz) large whole fish
   or 1 kg (2 lb 4 oz) fish fillets
2 teaspoons salt, plus extra, for
   sprinkling
olive oil, for brushing
1 lemon, thinly sliced
540 g (1 lb 3 oz/2 cups) tahini
185 ml (6 fl oz/¾ cup) lemon juice
1½ tablespoons olive oil
6 garlic cloves, crushed
1 handful coriander (cilantro) leaves,
   roughly chopped
2 long red chillies, seeded and roughly
   chopped, or 1 tablespoon chilli
   powder
155 g (5½ oz/1 cup) pine nuts, toasted
lemon wedges, to garnish, optional

For a whole fish, preheat the oven to 220°C (425°F/Gas 7). Sprinkle the fish with some salt 10 minutes before you use it. Brush the fish with oil and place the lemon slices in the cavity. Wrap it in foil, folding it tightly to seal. Bake for about 40 minutes. The fish should have a white flesh that is moist and easy to break into flaky pieces; if not, return it to the oven for a further 10 minutes.

For fish fillets, preheat the oven to 150°C (300°F/Gas 2). Brush the fish fillets with some oil and sprinkle with some salt. Place the lemon slices on top of the fish. Wrap it up in foil and bake for about 20 minutes or until the fish flesh is white, moist and easy to break into flaky pieces.

Meanwhile, blend the tahini, 1 teaspoon of the salt and half the lemon juice in a food processor. Add the rest of the lemon juice and combine. With the motor running, drizzle in up to 500 ml (17 fl oz/2 cups) of water to loosen the mixture. The tahini mixture should be semi-runny. Scoop into a bowl, then clean the food processor.

Place the garlic, coriander, chilli, if using, and the remaining 1 teaspoon salt in the food processor and pulse until chopped. Heat the oil in a non-stick frying pan over low heat and cook the garlic mixture for 5 minutes. Pour in the tahini sauce slowly while stirring. Keep stirring until it boils. If you are using chilli powder, add it now.

Carefully drain any liquid from the fish, remove the lemon from the cavity and lay the fish on a platter long and deep enough to fit the fish and hold the sauce.

Pour the tahini–chilli sauce over the fish. Garnish with pine nuts and serve with lemon wedges.

5

Citi Leila

Citi Leila's House

Where We Unite and Grow

> *'Mum's house is a place for everybody in the family. It doesn't matter what mood I am in, when I go there I feel comfort.'*
> Aunty Rosa

Our family gathering place has always been Citi's single-storey Federation home situated in the Sydney suburb of Dulwich Hill. The house has been central to most of the significant events that have shaped our lives. Once known as Gidi and Citi's house, since Gidi died in 2002, it is now referred to as Citi's house. A lot of effort was made to turn the house into the 'security hub' which as a family we are always drawn to. Citi's house has always brought us closer.

Citi's children and grandchildren celebrate traditional festivities there and have countless weekend barbecues in the backyard. Her door is open to each and every one of us. Aunty Rosa's wedding took place in the backyard with more than 300 guests. Aunty Therese's engagement party was basically held in the kitchen. The instant you enter the house you surrender to the love that continues to breed warmth and generosity. My aunties and uncles have grown up here and they have watched their children continue to grow here as well.

Gidi's honourable intentions of seeking to build a better life for his family meant that he had to live apart from Citi and the kids for ten years. Once he brought his wife and children over from Lebanon to live in their new home, he realised that time had created a wedge between them. He did his best to chip away at the awkward feeling of being a stranger to his own family and he worked hard to bring his children closer to him.

◆ **Citi Leila's House**

Living together again under the one roof as a family after ten years apart proved to be a challenge for Gidi and his children. 'The children were extremely shy towards their father,' explains Citi. 'They saw this man as a stranger to them and although they knew what the word Dad meant, they found it unusual to be in his presence.' My uncles and aunties were very young when Gidi left them and some of them could hardly remember him. 'It took a while for them to break through the comfort barrier. The children felt they had to be formal and courteous towards their father.' Citi remembers how they would constantly ask permission from her or their older sister Joumana for simple things such as a glass of water or a piece of fruit. She would have to reinforce for the children time and time again that this was their new life. They kept asking Citi, 'When is this man going back to his house? When are we going to return to where we came from?' She always responded, 'He is your father; this is our house and we all live together now.'

Gidi tried his best to make things more relaxed. When the children came home after school their mother was the first person who they would call for if they couldn't see her right away. 'Is Mum here?' they yelled, searching the rooms throughout the house. 'Mum, where are you?' Gidi would call back, 'I am here—your Dad is here.' Gidi struggled in those early years, and he often questioned whether it was worth the sacrifice that he made being away from them for such a long time. Citi explains, 'He would tell everyone and anyone to never leave their family like he did, no matter how poor they were.' Gidi would try to preach as much as he could the value of family. Citi says that often he would also say, 'What you eat and drink together shouldn't matter just as long as you have your family. Don't spend a minute without them.' Together Gidi and Citi did their best to raise their children; they worked hard to keep a roof over their heads and instil strong family values.

More than three hundred guests dined and danced under a huge white marquee that was set up in the backyard for Aunty Rosa's wedding in 1981. The backyard originally stretched to the next block before Uncle Joe built his two-storey brick house on half of it. Fresh flowers adorned the marquee, which was filled with enough hired tables, chairs and cutlery to accommodate all the guests for a sit-down feast. Almost anyone from Becharee who was living in Sydney was considered a 'relative' and therefore invited. Honour and dignity among the tight-knit community was displayed through setting up, cooking and celebrating together. 'Before I knew it, an army of people were at my door each day,' explains Citi. 'The hard work and dedication that came with preparing these large events was always a joyous journey, right from the beginning.' The men took charge of setting up, some of them sharing the task of running the six barbecues that cooked the meat on the day. The women spent the week leading up to the wedding in Citi's kitchen, helping her prepare traditional Lebanese dishes. Loyalty and support were expressed by stuffing hundreds of sambuskeh (see page 197), filling and rolling thousands of vine leaves (see page 199) and marinating kilogram upon kilogram of meat. Three lamb ouze (the entire carcass, skinned and with the head removed) were bought and stuffed with meat, rice, herbs and spices. They were then sewn up and sent to the local bakery that had a big enough oven to cook the entire animals. Citi has always emphasised to me that, 'we celebrate life through food, not just by eating together but by coming together and producing it.'

Fresh rose petals and rice showered Aunty Rosa and her husband Tony after the ceremony outside the church. The joy of such a sacred tradition was displayed through zhagareet carried out by some of the women. This involves producing wavering high-pitched sounds by vibrating the tongue against the roof of the mouth. Hands went in the air and waved from side to side, fingers clicking to the beat of the drum, feet breaking into the folk dance known as the dabkeh. When the formalities were over it was time to enjoy the celebrations. Trays of Lebanese sweets, chocolate and sugar-coated almonds wrapped in white mesh and tied with ribbon circulated through the dancing guests at the church ground. Then later in the backyard there was feasting and dancing until midnight.

A picture of sophistication on her engagement day, Aunty Therese wore a silk blouse splashed with shades of green and beige, neatly tucked in to a beige high-waisted silk pencil skirt. Her proud parents were delighted to have their daughter, the youngest of four sisters (the older three of whom were already married), heading in that direction. Citi explains that 'It's traditional for the parents of the bride to hold the engagement party at their house.' Unphased by the effort of holding an event like this, she says, 'We only had to cater for about seventy-plus adults and children; we had already held many bigger parties at the house by then. This one was a breeze.' Lebanese coffee and snacks were served in the formal lounge as the adults gathered for the official announcement and the placing of the engagement ring on the finger of Aunty Therese. 'This was the most nerve-wracking time for me,' admits Citi. 'I didn't know what to expect. The relatives from both sides of the families met for the first time in my not-so-big lounge room.' But that

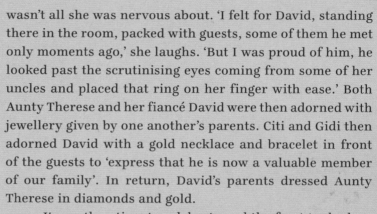

wasn't all she was nervous about. 'I felt for David, standing there in the room, packed with guests, some of them he met only moments ago,' she laughs. 'But I was proud of him, he looked past the scrutinising eyes coming from some of her uncles and placed that ring on her finger with ease.' Both Aunty Therese and her fiancé David were then adorned with jewellery given by one another's parents. Citi and Gidi then adorned David with a gold necklace and bracelet in front of the guests to 'express that he is now a valuable member of our family'. In return, David's parents dressed Aunty Therese in diamonds and gold.

It was then time to celebrate and the feast took place in the adjoining kitchen, dining and television rooms. The open non-partitioned spaces of all three rooms have proven beneficial for family gatherings over the years, especially when holding celebrations such as this. The usual furniture was moved aside to make way for tables covered in white sheets lined up across the three rooms to form an L-shape. We all sat comfortably, eating from the trays of food that were prepared by Citi and her daughters in the week leading up to the event.

Citi's house is not only the chosen venue for festivities but also a place where most of her children and grandchildren go to escape or when we are not feeling well. We have all sneaked up to her bedroom window in the early hours of the morning when a curfew had been broken. Three taps on the glass pane and she usually rolls herself out of bed, opens the door and gives a slight smirk and a wink. Before you know it, she has tucked you into bed. Safe and sound, sinking into one of her ever-so-comfortable mattresses, wrapped in one of her home-made doonas. As long as we were okay, our secrets were safe with her.

Without the house I don't think that we would be the family that we are. Citi's house belongs to all of us equally and she continues to make sure that it remains that way. When I have clashed with her, it has been over the cotton covers in garish colours that she makes to protect her sofas. To me they are eyesores that are only one step away from plastic covers, but to her they allow her children and grandchildren to sit, sleep or eat on her precious sofas. 'I don't want to compromise your comfort,' Citi always argues. 'I can cover them, let you enjoy them and when I want to be precious and want my house to look pretty I can take them off.' How could I ever argue with that?

'Citi's house offers security. I go there and feel secure and a sense of belonging. I have a strong attachment to the place. Every time I got sick, I'd pack the family and go to Mum's place. Mum was great at taking care of you.' Aunty Therese

'Citi's house is one of my favourite places; every time I go there I feel fourteen again—the same age when I first lived there with my father.'
My mother, Joumana

Shawarabat kishk

Kishk soup

serves 4

This makes an ideal winter soup, usually sipped for breakfast with broken crisp Lebanese bread added to the soup once it has been served.

25 g (1 oz) butter
1 onion, finely chopped
1 garlic clove, finely chopped
230 g (8 oz) minced (ground) lamb or
    beef, optional
130 g (4½ oz/1 cup) ready-made kishk
    granules (see Note)
Lebanese bread, to serve

Heat a deep-sided frying pan over low heat and add the butter. Once it is melted, add the onion and garlic and cook until soft. If you are adding meat, increase the heat to medium–high and cook it in the pan with the soft onion and garlic until it browns.

Add the kishk granules and 1 litre (35 fl oz/4 cups) of water. Bring to the boil and boil for 10 minutes, stirring from time to time. Make sure that all the lumps dissolve. The kishk should be a thin creamy soup.

You can either toast or leave the bread untoasted to have with the soup. If you would like it toasted, toast it briefly under a hot grill (broiler) or in the oven until crisp. You can break the crisp bread pieces into the soup once it has been served or you can dip the bread into the soup instead.

Note: Kishk is a dried, granular yoghurt available from Lebanese grocers.

The Making *of the* Kishk

Almost every summer as far back as I can remember Citi Leila has dedicated the hottest days to the laborious process of making kishk, which she then shares among her family.

Kishk is home-made fermented yoghurt (which we call laben, see page 30) that is mixed with crushed wheat (burghul) and turned into fine granules after days of roasting under the hot summer sun. The kishk is then stored until required to make the perfect thick, warming winter soup—it is added to boiling water and made flavoursome with onion, garlic and meat. Fresh or toasted Lebanese bread is usually broken up and added to the serving bowls. Meat-stuffed kibbab ovals are also boiled in the kishk soup to make Kibbab bi kishk (see page 125), which is another family favourite. Both of these dishes are usually served up for breakfast to beat the chills of winter.

During the week that the kishk is made or, as we excitedly like to call it, 'The making of the kishk', Citi's backyard is basically converted into a factory where the kishk is fermented and housed. Citi prefers to spend the first few days of the process preparing and fermenting on her own. She then calls on the rest of the family to knead the kishk into the final stage.

The journey for Citi begins by pouring many litres of milk and tubs of yoghurt into one of her oversized saucepans. She boils the milk and yoghurt

to make the laben, which she then hangs in cotton or muslin (cheesecloth) sacks outside in the fresh air for three days until all the fluid has drained away and just a creamy mixture remains.

On the fourth day, white cotton sheets are spread out to cover the concrete slab in her backyard. Narrow concrete pathways are left uncovered for us to tiptoe our way across the yard. The moist chunks of early-stage kishk are spread across the sheets and left to dry for a few hours before our hands are required. We always feel an overwhelming thrill on this day, despite the laborious task to come, surrounded by the thick pungent smell of the kishk. The spirit of youthfulness travels throughout the house and across the backyard where we are scattered either preparing ourselves for the task of kneading or where we have already begun. Scarfs and other material sewn together by Citi are wrapped around our heads. We make sure to expose our skin to the roasting summer sun. We talk and giggle for hours as we rub the thick kishk with the bottom of our wrists against the cotton over the concrete, turning it into fine granules. The rest of the week Citi relies on the sun to roast her kishk granules, turning it over now and then in order for it to thoroughly dry out. When it is all over, each family gets their share of the kishk, which is divided up into long glass jars that are then carefully stored, waiting for winter to arrive when we will use it to make soup.

Meeshee selh
Vegetarian silverbeet rolls
serves 6–8

1 kg (2 lb 4 oz/1 large bunch) silverbeet
(Swiss chard)
1–2 tomatoes, sliced
lemon wedges, to serve, optional

Stuffing
110 g (3¾ oz/½ cup) medium-grain
rice
2 onions, finely chopped
1 small handful flat-leaf (Italian)
parsley, finely chopped (reserve
the stems)
3 cooking tomatoes, diced, reserving
any juices
1 tablespoon mint, finely chopped
¾ teaspoon salt
½ teaspoon ground cumin
½ teaspoon finely ground Lebanese
black pepper
½ long red chilli, chopped or
⅛ teaspoon chilli powder
2 tablespoons olive oil

Wash the silverbeet, remove the stalks and slice the stalks into pieces. Set aside to use later. Blanch the leaves in boiling water until soft enough to roll without breaking. Drain. Lay each leaf with the textured side down. Use your fingers to crack the spine—this will loosen the leaf and make it easier to roll. Halve the leaf by cutting it with a knife widthways.

For the stuffing, soak the rice in hot water for up to 5 minutes. Strain and wash. Combine all of the ingredients in a strainer over a bowl. The liquid collected in the bowl will be used to cook the silverbeet rolls.

Cover the base of a large saucepan with the sliced tomato and then the reserved parsley stems.

Lay half a leaf on a flat work surface with the textured side facing up. Place 1 tablespoon of the filling in the middle of the leaf. Fold the sides in and tightly roll, then place in the saucepan. Repeat with the remaining leaves and filling. Stack the rolls tightly side by side and build layers of rolls.

Measure the liquid from the stuffing and add enough hot water to make up 250 ml (9 fl oz/1 cup) of liquid. Add to the pan and season with some salt. Lay a plate face down over the layers to keep them in place. Bring to the boil over high heat. Reduce the heat to low and cover with a lid. Simmer for 1½ hours, checking regularly.

If you like, serve with lemon wedges. The rolls can be eaten hot or cold; they are delicious with laben (see page 30), labneh (see page 31) or chilli sauce.

Kusa ma'a waraq inab
Stuffed zucchini with lamb chops and vine leaves
serves 8

Mum learnt this recipe from the other Lebanese women in the Australian community when she came to look after her father. When the rest of the family arrived, she taught the recipe to them.

500 g (1 lb 2 oz) preserved or 100 g
  (3½ oz) fresh vine leaves
1 kg (2 lb 4 oz/about 18) small
  Lebanese (pale green) zucchini
  (courgettes)
butter, for greasing
1 kg (2 lb 4 oz) lamb chops
3 cooking tomatoes, sliced
3 red or green capsicums (peppers),
  sliced
salt

Stuffing
220 g (7¾ oz/2 cups) medium-grain
  rice
2 brown onions, finely chopped
500 g (1 lb 2 oz/about 5) soft cooking
  tomatoes, chopped, reserving any
  juices
1 handful chopped mint
15 g (½ oz) butter
500 g (1 lb 2 oz) minced (ground) lamb
salt
¼ teaspoon chilli powder, optional
¼ teaspoon ground cinnamon
¼ teaspoon ground cumin
¼ teaspoon finely ground Lebanese
  black pepper

If you are using preserved leaves, wash them. If you are using fresh ones, blanch them in hot water until softened and dark green. Remove from the water and cut off the stems.

For the stuffing, soak the rice in hot water for up to 5 minutes. Strain and wash. Put the rice, onion, tomato and juices and mint in a sieve over a bowl to collect the liquid.

Melt the butter in a saucepan over high heat and add the meat. Cook, stirring, until the meat is broken up and cooked. Season with salt. Set aside to cool. Once cool, add the rice mixture along with the chilli, if using, and spices. Mix well.

Wash the zucchini and remove the tops. Using a zucchini scoop (manerah), start from the top and scrape out the pulp until only a thin layer of flesh is left on the inside walls of the zucchini. This is an artful task—if the mind wanders you create holes in the zucchini. Stuff the zucchini with the stuffing, leaving enough space for the filling to expand when it is cooking. My mum, to check if she has left enough space, sticks her index finger inside the zucchini; the empty space should be the same size as from the tip of her finger to her first knuckle.

Spread out each leaf, smooth-side down. Fill the centre of each leaf with about 1 tablespoon of stuffing. Bring the left and right sides of the leaf in first, then roll tightly to make a finger.

Lightly grease a frying pan with butter and cook the chops until browned on both sides. Cover the base of a large saucepan with tomato then layers of chops, capsicum, vine leaves and zucchini. Repeat layering, finishing with a layer of capsicum then tomato.

Measure the liquid from the stuffing and add enough hot water to make up 500 ml (17 fl oz/2 cups) of liquid. Add to the pan and season with salt. Lay a plate face down over the layers to keep them in place. Bring to the boil over high heat. Reduce the heat to low and cover with a lid. Simmer for 1½ hours.

Sumbuskeh
Minced meat and pine nut parcels

makes 35

vegetable oil, for deep-frying

Filling

3 teaspoons vegetable oil

1 brown onion, finely chopped

350 g (12 oz) minced (ground) lamb
  or beef

½ teaspoon salt

½ teaspoon my family's baharat spice
  mix (see page 22)

40 g (1½ oz/¼ cup) pine nuts

Dough

500 g (1 lb 2 oz) plain (all-purpose)
  flour

3 tablespoons vegetable oil

125 ml (4 fl oz/½ cup) beer

2 teaspoons sugar

1 teaspoon salt

For the filling, heat the oil in a frying pan over medium heat and cook the onion until soft and translucent. Set the onion aside in a bowl. Cook the meat in the pan, adding more oil, if required, and sprinkle with the salt and baharat. Cook the meat until browned and cooked through. Combine the meat with the onion in the bowl.

In a non-stick frying pan, cook the pine nuts until golden. Remove from the heat and combine with the onion and cooked meat. Season and set aside to cool completely.

For the dough, combine the ingredients and 125 ml (4 fl oz/½ cup) lukewarm water in a large bowl. Knead the dough and set aside in a lightly floured bowl. Cover with a damp cloth and rest for 30 minutes.

Sprinkle a work surface with flour. Divide the dough into four portions and work with one portion at a time. Using a rolling pin, roll the dough to about 3 mm (⅛ inch) thick. Cut out circles about 7 cm (2¾ inch) in diameter—you can use a cup, bowl or cutter to help you.

Place 1½ teaspoons of filling just off-centre of each dough circle. Fold the dough circles in half to form a semicircle pocket. To seal the parcels, use your fingers to pleat the edges. Alternatively, press the tines of a fork into the dough to crimp the edges.

Heat the oil in a saucepan to 180°C (350°F) and deep-fry the parcels in batches for 4 minutes, turning after 2 minutes, until golden on both sides. Drain on kitchen paper and serve. These are good with hummous (see page 38), babba ghanoush (see page 39) or labneh (see page 31).

Note: You can freeze uncooked parcels on trays lined with baking paper, making sure they are not touching each other. Frozen sumbuskeh will only need to be thawed for a short while, otherwise the dough will begin to cling and tear.

Coosa bi laben
Stuffed zucchini in yoghurt soup
serves 10–12

This is similar to the other stuffed zucchini recipes, but in this version, toasted pine nuts are used instead of vegetables.

Stuffing

1 tablespoon vegetable oil

115 g (4 oz/¾ cup) pine nuts

110 g (3¾ oz/½ cup) medium-grain rice

2 brown onions, finely chopped

15 g (½ oz) butter

500 g (1 lb 2 oz) minced (ground) lamb or beef with no fat

salt

¼ teaspoon ground cinnamon

¼ teaspoon ground cumin

¼ teaspoon finely ground Lebanese black pepper

1 kg (2 lb 4 oz/about 18) small Lebanese (pale green) zucchini (courgettes)

4 garlic cloves

½ teaspoon dried mint

1½ teaspoons salt

1.5 litres (52 fl oz/6 cups) plain yoghurt or home-made laben (see page 32)

1 egg

1 teaspoon cornflour (cornstarch)

For the stuffing, heat the oil in a frying pan over medium heat and add the nuts. Cook, stirring, until golden. Set aside.

Soak the rice in hot water for up to 5 minutes. Strain and wash. Put the rice, onion and pine nuts in a bowl and set aside.

Melt the butter in a saucepan over high heat and add the meat. Cook, stirring, until the meat is broken up and cooked. Season with salt. Set aside to cool. Once cool, add to the rice mixture along with the cinnamon, cumin and pepper. Mix well.

Wash the zucchini and remove the tops. Using a zucchini scoop (manerah), start from the top and scrape out the pulp until only a thin layer of flesh is left on the inside walls of the zucchini. This is an artful task—if the mind wanders you create holes in the zucchini. Put the zucchini and salt in a bowl and cover with cold water. Leave to soak for about 5 minutes—this will soften it for cooking.

Stuff the zucchini with the stuffing, leaving enough space for the filling to expand when it is cooking. My mum, to check if she has left enough space, sticks her index finger inside the zucchini; the empty space should be the same size as from the tip of her finger to her first knuckle.

Boil 3 litres (105 fl oz/12 cups) of water in a saucepan. Add the zucchini and boil for 30 minutes.

Crush the garlic and mint with a little of the salt using a mortar and pestle until silken. With an electric beater, beat the yoghurt, egg, cornflour and remaining salt until combined and runny. Stir the mint and garlic paste into the pot with the water and zucchini. Continue to boil, stirring, for 5 minutes. Pour in the yoghurt mixture while continuing to stir. Once the soup has returned to the boil, it is ready to serve. To keep leftover soup, allow to cool completely, uncovered, then store in an airtight container in the fridge.

Waraq inab
Stuffed vine leaves

serves 6–8

500 g (1 lb 2 oz) preserved or 100 g
  (3½ oz) fresh vine leaves
1–2 tomatoes, sliced

Stuffing
220 g (7¾ oz/1 cup) medium-grain rice
2 tablespoons mint, finely chopped
½ bunch handful flat-leaf (Italian)
  parsley, finely chopped (reserve
  the stems)
1 kg (2 lb 4 oz) soft cooking tomatoes,
  finely diced, reserving any juices
4 onions, finely chopped
2 teaspoons salt
¼ teaspoon chilli powder
1 teaspoon ground cumin
1 teaspoon finely ground Lebanese
  black pepper
juice of 2 lemons
4 tablespoons olive oil

If you are using preserved leaves, wash them. If you are using fresh ones, blanch them in hot water until softened and dark green. Remove from the water and cut off the stems.

For the stuffing, soak the rice in hot water for up to 5 minutes. Strain and wash. Combine all of the ingredients in a strainer over a bowl. The liquid collected in the bowl will be used to cook the vine leaf rolls.

Cover the base of a saucepan with the sliced tomato and then the reserved parsley stems.

Spread out each leaf, smooth-side down. Depending on the size of the leaf, place 2 teaspoons to 1 tablespoon of the stuffing towards the base of the leaf. Bring the left and right sides of the leaf in first, then roll up tightly to make a finger. Place in the saucepan. Repeat with the remaining leaves and filling. Stack the rolls tightly side by side and build layers of rolls.

Measure the liquid from the stuffing and add enough hot water to make 500 ml (17 fl oz/2 cups) of liquid. Add to the pan and season with salt. Lay a plate face down over the layers to keep them in place. Bring to the boil over high heat. Reduce the heat to low and cover with a lid. Simmer for about 1½ hours. Serve the vine leaves warm or cold the next day.

Meeshee malfouf bi lahem

Cabbage rolls stuffed with meat

serves 6–8

1 large white cabbage
1–2 large tomatoes, sliced
lemon wedges, to serve, optional

Stuffing
440 g (15½ oz/2 cups) medium-grain
    rice
80 g (2¾ oz) butter
500 g (1 lb 2 oz) minced (ground)
    lamb or beef
2 teaspoons salt
3 onions, finely chopped
⅓ cup fresh mint, chopped, or
    1 teaspoon dried mint
6 garlic cloves, crushed
2 teaspoons ground cinnamon
2 teaspoons finely ground Lebanese
    black pepper
½ long red chilli or ⅛ teaspoon chilli
    powder

Separate the leaves of the cabbage and add to a large saucepan of boiling water. Cook until the leaves are limp and soft enough to roll. Transfer to a colander over a bowl to drain. Cut the bottom stem off the leaves and carve out the hard middle on the back of each leaf. Keep the hard bits to use later. The bigger leaves can be cut into four pieces and the medium ones into two pieces.

For the stuffing, soak the rice in hot water for up to 5 minutes. Strain and wash. Put into a strainer over a bowl.

Melt the butter in a saucepan over high heat and add the meat. Cook, stirring, until the meat is broken up and cooked. Season with the salt. Add to the strainer with the rice, along with all the other stuffing ingredients. The juice collected in the bowl will be used to cook the cabbage rolls.

Cover the base of the saucepan with the hard bits from the leaves followed by the tomato slices.

Lay a leaf on a work surface with the textured side facing up. Place 1 tablespoon of the mixture in the middle of the leaf. Fold the sides in and tightly roll, then place in the pan. Repeat with the remaining leaves and filling. Stack the rolls tightly side by side and build layers of rolls.

Measure the liquid from the stuffing and add enough hot water to make up 500 ml (17 fl oz/2 cups) of liquid. Add to the pan and season with salt. Lay a plate face down over the layers to keep them in place. Bring to the boil over high heat. Reduce the heat to low and cover with a lid. Simmer for about 1½ hours.

If you like, serve with lemon wedges. The rolls can be eaten hot or cold; they are delicious with laben (see page 30), labneh (see page 31) or chilli sauce.

Meeshee malfouf
Vegetarian cabbage rolls
serves 6–8

The entire leaf is always used when making stuffed cabbage rolls. Although the stem or stalk are cut off from the leaves they are used as the foundation to lay the stuffed rolls on. The juice from the vegetables is also essential to keep in order to cook the rolls in. It's about utilising every part of the food that you are cooking with.

1 large white or green cabbage
1–2 large tomatoes, sliced
lemon wedges, to serve, optional

Stuffing
330 g (11½ oz/1½ cups) medium-grain rice
500 g (1 lb 2 oz) soft cooking tomatoes, finely diced, reserving any juices
1 big handful flat-leaf (Italian) parsley, finely chopped
2 tablespoon mint leaves, finely chopped, or 1 teaspoon dried mint
2½ onions, finely chopped
6 garlic cloves, finely chopped
2½ tablespoons olive oil
1 tablespoon ground cumin
2 teaspoons salt
⅛ teaspoon chilli powder

Separate the leaves of the cabbage and add to a large saucepan of boiling water. Cook until the leaves are limp and soft enough to roll. Transfer to a colander over a bowl to drain. Cut off the stems and carve out the hard middle on the back of each leaf. Keep the hard bits to use later. The bigger leaves can be cut into four pieces and the medium ones into two pieces.

For the stuffing, soak the rice in hot water for up to 5 minutes. Strain and wash. Combine all of the ingredients in a strainer over a bowl. The liquid collected in the bowl will be used to cook the cabbage rolls.

Lay a leaf on a work surface with the textured side facing up. Place 1 tablespoon of the mixture in the middle of the leaf. Fold the sides in and tightly roll up, then place in the saucepan. Repeat with the remaining leaves and filling. Stack the rolls tightly side by side and build layers of rolls.

Measure the liquid from the stuffing and add enough hot water to make up 500 ml (17 fl oz/2 cups) of liquid. Add to the pan and season with salt. Lay a plate face down over the layers to keep them in place. Bring to the boil over high heat. Reduce the heat to low and cover with a lid. Simmer for about 1½ hours.

If you like, serve with lemon wedges. The rolls can be eaten hot or cold; they are delicious with laben (see page 30), labneh (see page 31) or chilli sauce.

Lahem bi ageen
Mini Lebanese pizzas

makes 22

vegetable oil, for brushing

Dough
750 g (1 lb 10 oz/5 cups) plain
   (all-purpose) flour, plus extra,
   for brushing
1 tablespoon active dry yeast
1 teaspoon salt
3 teaspoons sugar
125 ml (4 fl oz/½ cup) olive oil
⅛ teaspoon mahlab (aromatic spice,
   see page 22), finely pounded

Topping
350 g (12 oz) minced (ground) lamb
350 g (12 oz) soft cooking tomatoes,
   finely chopped
2 brown onions, finely chopped
1 small red capsicum (pepper), finely
   chopped
¾ teaspoon my family's baharat spice
   mix (see page 22)
¾ teaspoon salt
⅛ teaspoon chilli powder, optional

For the dough, combine all of the ingredients and 375 ml
(13 fl oz/1½ cups) lukewarm water, then knead for 5 minutes,
or until you have a manageable dough. Set aside and cover with
a kitchen towel for 1 hour, or until it rises.

Preheat the oven to 200°C (400°F/Gas 6). For the topping,
combine all the ingredients in a bowl and mix using your
hands. Make sure the vegetables and seasoning are evenly
spread through the meat.

Tear out a chunk of dough about the size of an egg. Use the
tips of your fingers and hands to flatten and shape the dough
into a circle on a work surface dusted with flour. Continue
until you make a thin circle about 12 cm (4½ inches) in
diameter. Repeat until you have used up all the dough.

Brush three baking trays with oil and place the pizza
dough bases onto the trays. Spread 1½ tablespoons of the meat
topping on each base. Using your fingers, make small folds
around the edge of the dough base, pinching the edges. Brush
the tops with a little oil. Cook for about 20 minutes, or until
golden and the bases are crisp.

Manoushet za'atar
Za'atar pizzas
makes 8

This pizza is the same as the Mini Lebanese pizzas on the opposite page only here you are using za'atar and oil on the dough. You will need to cook these pizzas in batches of two or three.

1 quantity Mini Lebanese pizza dough
   (see opposite page)
plain (all-purpose) flour, for dusting
125 ml (4 fl oz/½ cup) olive oil
50 g (1¾ oz/½ cup) my family's za'atar
   (see page 63)

Preheat the oven to 200°C (400°F/Gas 6). Tear out a chunk of dough about the size of a tennis ball. Dust a work surface with flour. Use a rolling pin to roll out to a 22 cm (8½ inch) diameter round.

Brush a baking tray with a little oil and place the pizza dough base on the tray. Make finger imprints in the base—this forms tiny catchment areas for concentrated amounts of the topping to sit in.

Combine the oil and za'atar. Brush a little of this mixture over the pizza base. Bake for 10 minutes, or until golden. Repeat with the remaining dough and za'atar mixture.

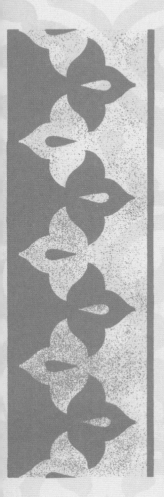

Znood il sit

Lady fingers

makes about 40

Filling

20 g (¾ oz) butter

2 brown onions, finely chopped

500 g (1 lb 2 oz) minced (ground) topside lamb or beef shoulder

¼ teaspoon salt

1 teaspoon my family's baharat spice mix (see page 22)

50 g (1¾ oz/⅓ cup) pine nuts

10 filo pastry sheets

3 tablespoons vegetable oil, for brushing

Preheat the oven to 220°C (425°F/Gas 7).

For the filling, melt half of the butter in a saucepan over low heat and cook the onion until soft and translucent. Remove from the pan and set aside in a bowl. Increase the heat to high and cook the meat with the remaining butter, salt and baharat until the meat is browned and cooked. Add to the onion.

In a non-stick frying pan, cook the pine nuts until golden brown. Remove from the heat and combine the pine nuts with the onion and cooked meat. Set aside to cool completely.

Brush two baking trays with oil. Working with one sheet of pastry at a time, cut the pastry into four equal strips of 11.5 x 28 cm (4¼ x 11¼ inches). Lift the shorter edge of each strip and fold it over to join the opposite edge, so you end up with a double layer of pastry that is 11.5 × 14 cm (4¼ x 5½ inches). Lay the pastry so the short side is closest to you.

Place 1 tablespoon of the filling on the pastry at the end closest to you. Fold the side flaps in towards the middle and begin to gently roll up from the short end. Dampen your fingers slightly with water and dab the end to seal.

Place the rolls side by side on the baking tray. Brush some of the oil on the top of the rolls. Bake for 15–20 minutes, or until the rolls are golden brown.

Meeshee coosa
Stuffed zucchini in tomato soup

serves 10–12

You can use minced lamb or beef but ask the butcher for no fat. Use topside beef or lamb from the leg for the best results.

Stuffing

110 g (3¾ oz/½ cup) medium-grain
   rice

2 brown onions, finely chopped

5 soft cooking tomatoes, chopped,
   reserving any juices

1 handful chopped fresh mint or
   1 teaspoon dried mint

15 g (½ oz) butter

salt

500 g (1 lb 2 oz) minced (ground)
   topside beef

¼ teaspoon chilli powder, optional

½ teaspoon ground cinnamon

½ teaspoon ground cumin

½ teaspoon finely ground Lebanese
   black pepper

2 kg (4 lb 8 oz/about 36) small
   Lebanese (pale green) zucchini
   (courgettes)

¼ teaspoon salt

3 tablespoons tomato paste
   (concentrated purée)

juice of 2 lemons

For the stuffing, soak the rice in hot water for up to 5 minutes. Strain and wash. Put the rice, onion, tomato and mint in a sieve over a bowl to collect the liquid for later.

Melt the butter in a saucepan over high heat and add the meat. Cook, stirring, until the meat is broken up and cooked. Season with salt. Set aside to cool. Once cool, add the rice mixture along with the chilli, if using, and spices. Mix well.

Wash the zucchini and remove the tops. Using a zucchini scoop (manerah), start from the top and scrape out the pulp until only a thin layer of flesh is left on the inside walls of the zucchini. This is an artful task—if the mind wanders you create holes in the zucchini. Put the zucchini and salt in a bowl and cover with cold water, then soak for about 5 minutes—this will soften it for cooking.

Stuff the zucchini with the stuffing, leaving enough space for the filling to expand when it is cooking. My mum, to check if she has left enough space, sticks her index finger inside the zucchini; the empty space should be the same size as from the tip of her finger to her first knuckle.

Measure the liquid collected from the stuffing and add enough water to make up 4 litres (140 fl oz/16 cups). Pour it into an 8 litre (280 fl oz/32 cup) saucepan. Bring the liquid to the boil. Drop the zucchini into the boiling liquid and cook for 15 minutes. Add the tomato paste and lemon juice and stir until the tomato paste dissolves. Reduce the heat to low, then cover with a lid. Simmer for about 1 hour.

Notes: If there is any of the stuffing left over, add it to the water when you drop in the zucchini—the result will be a rustic soup. Use the zucchini pulp to make the Zucchini omelettes (see page 28).

Fatayr
Triangle spinach pies

makes 22

vegetable oil, for brushing

Dough
750 g (1 lb 10 oz/5 cups) plain
   (all-purpose) flour
1 tablespoon active dry yeast
1 teaspoon salt
3 teaspoons sugar
125 ml (4 fl oz/½ cup) olive oil
⅛ teaspoon mulhub (aromatic spice,
   see page 22)
125 ml (4 fl oz/½ cup) lukewarm milk

Filling
1 kg (2 lb 4 oz/1 large bunch) silverbeet
   (Swiss chard) or English spinach,
   washed and drained well
1 teaspoon salt
2 brown onions, finely chopped
3 tablespoons olive oil
2 teaspoons sumac or juice of ½ lemon
200 g (7 oz/1⅓ cups) crumbled feta
   cheese, optional

For the dough, combine all of the ingredients and 250 ml (9 fl oz/1 cup), then knead for 5 minutes until you have a manageable dough. Set aside and cover with a kitchen towel for 1 hour, or until it rises.

Preheat the oven to 200°C (400°F/Gas 6). For the filling, slice off all of stalks of the silverbeet, leaving just the leaf. Finely shred the leaves and add to a bowl with the salt. Use your hands to tightly squeeze the silverbeet to remove any moisture. Add the rest of the filling ingredients and mix well.

Tear out a chunk of dough about the size of an egg. Flatten and shape using your hands and the tips of your fingers. Continue until you make a thin circle that is about 13 cm (5 inches) in diameter.

In the middle of the dough circle, place 2 tablespoons of the filling. Fold the dough, bringing three points together to form a triangle shape. Pinch the edges of the dough tightly to seal. Repeat with the remaining dough circles and filling.

Brush a baking tray with vegetable oil. Place the pies on the tray and brush the tops with a little oil. Bake for 20–30 minutes, or until golden brown.

6
Aunty Therese
And Now
for Dessert

Hope You've Left Some Room for Sweets

'Coffee cup reading is the Lebanese version of reading your horoscope.'
Aunty Therese

The ritual of brewing and drinking Lebanese coffee remains an integral part of the way we socialise. It is used as a way of welcoming guests, and coffee is poured throughout the day. The strong black coffee is often made in a rakweh, a long-handled pot. It is served on a tray and poured in front of guests in a demitasse (espresso) cup that sits on a saucer. The rich sediment (tefl) that remains at the bottom of the cup after the coffee has been drunk has always been cherished for the messages it leaves. It is believed that these symbols can be interpreted by a gifted coffee-cup reader.

Aunty Therese was seven years old when she had her first coffee cup read. Desperate to know her destiny, the opportunity presented itself one afternoon when one of the older women from the village popped over. 'I will never forget my first reading, it was done by one of our favourite neighbours, who would usually come over and entertain us with her cup readings,' Aunty Therese explains. 'We would huddle around her eager, to hear what she had to say.' Aunty Therese struck a deal with her mother and offered to make coffee for the first time without her mother's assistance as long as she was allowed to drink some and have her cup read. Citi Leila agreed but stressed that she must remember the coffee-making method she had been taught. 'I know, I know, Mum,' Aunty Therese answered, eager to get on with it. 'I reduce the heat once it starts to boil.' 'And what else?' her mother asked her as if it was a test. 'I have to allow it to simmer until the foam turns into bubbles and, once the bubbles disappear, it's ready,' came the answer. Standing on a stool and leaning over the stove, she carefully stirred in the coffee grains. She remembers how she was transfixed by the grains as they swirled. 'I felt thrilled by the mysticism and the power these grains held,' she tells me. The thought that her destiny would soon be revealed made her heart dance. 'There was so much I was anticipating hearing.'

Once the coffee was made, she served the ladies and proceeded to pour a few drops for herself. After taking a sip, 'I looked at the bottom of my cup and began to swirl the remainder of the liquid and sediment, proud of myself for remembering to keep just enough at the bottom.' She covered the cup with a saucer and tipped it upside down for a few minutes. 'I wanted the liquid and sediment to spread out as much as possible'. Aunty Therese was adamant that by doing this, 'there would be more of the future to see'. The older woman looked into her cup and said: 'Your mother is going to buy you a pretty dress with big ribbons.' That was it. Aunty Therese had nothing to respond with 'except a look of sheer disappointment,' she recalls. 'That's not what I wanted to hear. I didn't want a dress, I was content in my jeans and T-shirt.' She felt cheated. She persuaded the neighbour to do a second read, and this time the woman said, in an exaggerated cutesy voice, 'it's going to be the prettiest dress you have ever seen'. Hearing about that dress again gave Aunty Therese a knot in her stomach. 'What I was hoping to hear,' she explains, 'was that I was going to travel to faraway places, that I was going to go on an adventure just like my older sister.' She also had a deep yearning to see her father who was living in Australia at the time.

There is no science behind how cups are read. It can be argued that a good reader is an intuitive one, someone who is capable of tapping into what a person is feeling and

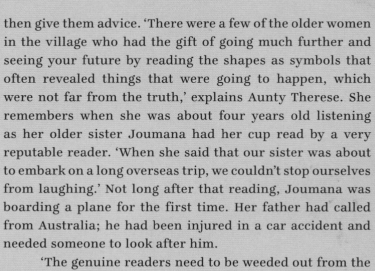

then give them advice. 'There were a few of the older women in the village who had the gift of going much further and seeing your future by reading the shapes as symbols that often revealed things that were going to happen, which were not far from the truth,' explains Aunty Therese. She remembers when she was about four years old listening as her older sister Joumana had her cup read by a very reputable reader. 'When she said that our sister was about to embark on a long overseas trip, we couldn't stop ourselves from laughing.' Not long after that reading, Joumana was boarding a plane for the first time. Her father had called from Australia; he had been injured in a car accident and needed someone to look after him.

'The genuine readers need to be weeded out from the frauds,' according to Aunty Therese, and she developed a knack for doing just that. 'Growing up in a tight-knit community in Sydney had its perks, but as a teenage girl I wanted my own privacy and individuality,' Aunty Therese explains. Conveniently for the young teenager, one of the neighbours gave herself away one too many times during a coffee-cup-reading session. After realising her motives early on, Aunty Therese turned the situation around to her advantage. She insisted on having the gossip queen read her cup. 'It was obvious that the cup was a ploy to investigate what I had been getting up to,' she explains. 'Knowing things like what time I had been getting home late at night was a dead give-away that she had been snooping. I was cheeky, but I was protective of my privacy at the same time.'

The excruciating wait for her final exam results was taxing on the eighteen-year-old, who was also dealing with 'gentlemen' callers. Although she was considered to be of prime marriageable age, she was operating on a different timeframe. 'The push to have me married became clear during coffee-cup readings, especially from the mothers with sons they wanted me to consider,' she explains, rolling her eyes and shaking her head. 'All I heard during that time was that the right one was coming. Damn the right one coming, I thought, I am not waiting for the right one. All I wanted was someone who could look into that cup and tell me that I was going to get the marks that would get me to university to study psychology.' Although none of her readings came up with that information, Aunty Therese did fulfil her dream of studying psychology. The 'one' to whom she would be married did come, but much later on.

Aunty Therese remembers being inspired as a young child listening to a wise old lady read things in her mother's cup. She explains by imitating the old reader: 'You are going to have one child that will save you. One who will not allow you to get into ruin.' She adds, 'That stuck in my mind, I always wanted to be the one to fulfil that role.' From that day on, she was intent on being that child.

It's questionable whether the old lady saw something in Aunty Therese's cup that day, or whether she saw something in the relationship between mother and daughter that she felt compelled to express. Either way, Aunty Therese explains that, 'sometimes cup reading by adults for children and young adults is used as a tool for them to reach out and tell them things they couldn't otherwise.' The valued art of the reader is therefore not just what they can see in the cup but also how they use the cup to connect with others. 'Everybody likes to delve into the unknown; it's very entertaining,' explains Aunty Therese, 'but we also get an insight into each other's lives, which is very important.'

Njuz mkhutus bil atter
Citi Leila's pears dipped in atter

fills a 2 litre (70 fl oz) jar

1 kg (2 lb 4 oz) ripe small pears, skin
   on, stems attached
880 g (1 lb 15 oz/4 cups) sugar

Wash and dry the pears.

Place the sugar and 500 ml (17 fl oz/2 cups) of water in a saucepan over low heat, stirring to dissolve the sugar. Increase the heat to high and boil for 7 minutes, or until syrupy.

Place a few pears at a time into the hot syrup and simmer for 2 minutes, then transfer them to a 2 litre (70 fl oz/8 cup) sterilised jar.

Pour the remainder of the hot syrup into the jar and allow to cool down before fitting the lid. Store for up to 2 weeks.

Atter
Sugar syrup

makes 500 ml (17 fl oz)

This syrup is used on most of the desserts in this book.

460 g (1 lb) caster (superfine) sugar
1½ teaspoons lemon juice
3 small thin pieces of lemon rind,
   pith removed

Place the sugar, lemon juice and rind and 250 ml (9 fl oz/1 cup) of water in a small saucepan over low heat, stirring to dissolve the sugar. Once the sugar is dissolved, stop stirring, increase the heat to high and bring to the boil. Reduce the heat to low and simmer for 8 minutes, or until slightly syrupy. The syrup is ready once the lemon rind is translucent and starting to curl at the edges. Remove from the heat and set aside to cool. Remove the lemon rind.

Pour the syrup into a sterilised jar and allow to cool down before fitting the lid. Store for up to 2 months in the fridge.

Foosteeyeah

Sesame and peanut slice

makes 24

vegetable oil, for brushing
1 kg (2 lb 4 oz) raw peanuts with
  no skin
500 g (1 lb 2 oz) sesame seeds
500 g (1 lb 2 oz) honey
2 tablespoons icing (confectioners')
  sugar, sifted

Preheat the oven to 160°C (315°F/Gas 2–3). Lightly grease a 35 × 25 × 2.5 cm (14 × 10 × 1 inch) metal tray with oil.

Place the peanuts on two baking trays and roast for 15–20 minutes. Keep an eye on them—they will need to be tossed so that they roast on all sides.

Meanwhile, toast the sesame seeds in a non-stick frying pan. Constantly stir until golden brown. Place the peanuts and sesame seeds in a large bowl.

Put the honey and icing sugar in a saucepan over low heat, stirring until melted and combined. Increase the heat and bring to the boil. Cook the mixture until it reaches 116°C (241°F/soft ball stage) on a candy thermometer.

Pour the hot honey mixture over the peanuts and sesame seeds. Working quickly, stir to combine then pour into the prepared tray. With the back of a spoon, press the top of the mixture to spread it out evenly. Set aside to cool for 2–3 hours. Cut into squares and serve.

Note: You can use any nuts for this dish.

Tumr malfoofeh
Date rolls
makes 40

1 kg (2 lb 4 oz) pitted soft Lebanese
   dates
100 g (3½ oz) plain sweet biscuits
   (cookies), broken into small pieces
200 g (7 oz/2 cups) walnuts, roughly
   chopped
120 g (4¼ oz/2 cups) desiccated
   coconut

Wash the dates, then put them in a saucepan with 250 ml
(9 fl oz/1 cup) of water over medium heat. When the mixture
comes to the boil, reduce the heat to low and mash until the
dates become jam-like. Transfer to a bowl and cool completely.

Add the biscuit pieces and walnuts to the dates and mix well.

Scatter the coconut on a work surface. Roll the date mixture
into four long logs about 7 cm (2¾ inch) in diameter. Roll in
the scattered coconut until well covered.

Wrap the logs in foil and refrigerate overnight. The logs can
then be cut into slices and served.

Tumr bi lawz ma'a chocolat
Chocolate-covered dates stuffed with almonds
makes 20

20 fresh large dates
50 g (1¾ oz/⅓ cup) blanched almonds
200 g (7 oz) dark chocolate
   (70% cocoa), chopped
very finely grated zest of 1 orange
1 tablespoon pistachio kernels, finely
   crushed

Hold a date in one hand and use a thin fork handle to push
the pit out, keeping the shape of the date as intact as possible.
Discard the pit; repeat with the remaining dates. Press two
almonds into each date. Bring a saucepan of water to the boil,
then reduce to a simmer. Put the chocolate in a heatproof bowl
over the water (ensuring the base of the bowl is not in contact
with the water). Heat the chocolate, stirring gently until melted
and smooth. Stir in the orange zest. Remove from the heat.

One at a time add a date to the chocolate and, using two
forks, coat in the chocolate, draining off any excess. Place on a
wire rack over a tray and sprinkle with the crushed pistachios.
Repeat with the remaining dates. Refrigerate for 2 hours to set
the chocolate, then serve straight from the fridge.

Atayef mishi bi jowez oh foostah halabee

Lebanese pancakes stuffed with nuts

makes 20

2 teaspoons (7 g) active dry yeast
300 g (10½ oz/2 cups) plain
   (all-purpose) flour
2 tablespoons sugar
vegetable oil, for greasing
sugar syrup, at room temperature,
   for drizzling (see page 222)

Nut filling
135 g (4¾ oz/1⅓ cups) walnuts
200 g (7 oz/1⅓ cups) pistachio kernels
1¼ teaspoons orange blossom water
100 g (3½ oz) sugar

Ashta filling, optional
ashta (Lebanese clotted cream) or
   thick (double) cream (see Note)

Dissolve the yeast in 2 tablespoons of warm water. Sift the flour into a bowl and add the yeast, sugar and 625 ml (21½ fl oz/2½ cups) of warm water. Using an electric beater, beat until you have a runny mixture. Set aside and cover with a kitchen towel for 1 hour, or until it rises.

For the nut filling, place the nuts in a food processor and pulse twice. Transfer the nuts to a bowl with the orange blossom water and sugar and mix together.

Grease a non-stick or cast-iron frying pan with ¼ teaspoon oil and heat over medium heat. Pour ⅓ cup of the batter into the frying pan. Spread the batter to make a round pancake about 12 cm (4½ inches) in diameter. Cook one side until lightly golden. The top should begin to form small craters or holes; once the top dries, remove the pancake from the heat, do not flip over. Repeat with the remaining batter.

Place each pancake on a work surface, holey-side up. Place about 1 tablespoon of filling just off-centre of each pancake. Fold the pancake in half and press the edges together to seal. Drizzle with syrup and serve at room temperature.

Note: You can fill the pancakes with either nuts or ashta. Either way the syrup is always drizzled on top. Ashta is Lebanese clotted cream, typically made by reducing full-cream (whole) milk. It is available from Lebanese grocers.

Ma'mool
Walnut and date biscuits

makes 50

The tamar, tamreah or oleb il mamoul is used to mould these biscuits. My family use the tamar that has two different wooden engravings on the dome—the different markings are to distinguish between the date biscuits and the walnut ones. It doesn't matter which print is used for which.

Dough

500 g (1 lb 2 oz) unsalted butter

500 g (1 lb 2 oz) coarse semolina, plus extra

500 g (1 lb 2 oz) fine semolina

110 g (3¾ oz/½ cup) white sugar

1 teaspoon mahlab (aromatic spice, see page 22)

1 teaspoon ground aniseed powder

½ teaspoon active dry yeast

1 tablespoon rosewater

125 ml (4 fl oz/½ cup) orange blossom water, plus 1½ tablespoons, extra

350 g (12 oz/3½ cups) walnuts

110 g (3¾ oz/½ cup) white sugar

700 g (1 lb 9 oz) Lebanese date purée, mashed, at room temperature

icing (confectioners') sugar, for dusting

For the dough, melt the butter in a saucepan over low heat; remove the pan from the heat as soon as it has melted. In a large bowl combine the semolina and sugar and mix together with your hands. Add the mahlab and aniseed powder and mix through. Dissolve the yeast in 1 tablespoon of lukewarm water. Mix into the semolina mixture. Pour in the rosewater and orange blossom water and mix well. Start kneading the dough and slowly begin to pour in the melted butter. Keep kneading until the dough is soft, silky, and glistening from the butter—you may need to add an extra few tablespoons of semolina. Set the dough aside in a bowl covered with a cloth at room temperature. The dough needs to rest for a minimum of 3 hours and up to 24 hours.

Preheat the oven to 150°C (300°F/Gas 2). Line two baking trays with baking paper. Pulse a handful of the walnuts at a time so they are still a little chunky. Scoop into a bowl and combine with the white sugar.

Add the extra orange blossom water to the dough and knead for 5 minutes. Fill a bowl with warm water to wet your hands.

Tear out a small chunk of dough and roll into a 4 cm (1½ inch) diameter ball between the palms of your hands. Poke through one end of the ball to hollow out a pocket. Work your finger around to create a thin wall. Fill the pocket with 1 tablespoon of either walnuts or dates. Close it up. Press the dough ball into the concave dome of the tamar. Flatten the exposed base of the dough using your hand. Turn the tamar over, hit the tip against a hard surface and catch the dough dome with your other hand. Put on the prepared tray. Repeat.

Bake for 30–35 minutes, or until the biscuits turn the colour of pale honeycomb. Cool on wire racks. Once cooled, sift icing sugar over the walnut biscuits; leave the date ones plain.

The Secret *of* Arak

Although I have shared many of my family's secret recipes with you, I do have to stop somewhere. After some deliberation with my brother I have decided that the recipe for our sacred family brew, arak, will be protected, as befits a family treasure. Arak is the national alcoholic drink of Lebanon and it is made from green grapes and flavoured with aniseed.

The process and measurements that my family follow when making this ouzo-like spirit is unique to them. Only a few of us from the inner sanctum know the precise measurements and temperature for making arak. I haven't yet been given the honour of the secret recipe. However, stories told to me by Citi and the family, usually after a few shots of arak have been consumed, have enabled me to muster up the basic details of the way in which this precious liqueur was made back in Lebanon.

So the story goes like this: at the end of each grape season in September or October, the well-ripened grapes and their vines were picked and placed into large barrels for one month in order to break down and ferment. During this time the grapes had to be stirred twice a week in order to release the trapped gases.

The next step was to purify the fermented grapes, which meant the arak makers had to extract as much liquid as possible from the decaying fruit. Using their hands, they sifted the grapes through a large colander-type instrument made from mesh that was tightly framed by wood. It was important that only the liquid and no decay went through the mesh and into the wooden box that sat underneath, otherwise the liquid would have to be poured out and sifted through again.

Long round sterilised barrels were then filled to hold the purified liquid for three weeks. The

barrels were stored in a dark, well ventilated room during this time.

The instrument used to distil the liquid is called the karkeh. It is made out of clay in the shape of a gigantic pear capable of holding about 50 litres of liquid. Enough of the purified liquid was poured in to half-fill the karkeh and it was then boiled until it reached the family's secret temperature. Once this temperature was reached, water and aniseed were added.

Four dedicated arak makers from the village were required to share the task of monitoring the temperature and refilling the karkeh. Two workers were on duty during the night while the other two monitored throughout the day. This would go on for four days, until all the liquid had vapourised through the karkeh.

Once all the liquid in the karkeh evaporated, it was cleaned up and the process had to begin all over again.

The delicate process of making arak also translates into the way that we drink it. Before it can be consumed the right procedure of mixing it together has to be followed—if you don't, it crystallises up the top and you can't drink it. The method is to pour one-third quantity of arak into a short glass, then add two-thirds water followed by some ice cubes. If the water is added first, you've wasted this precious drop.

Arak should only be consumed with a heavy meal or banquet. It is ideal with raw meat. Arak is never consumed with other spirits or fruit.

'Khaleena' (may we stay together) is the greeting and exchange between people before the first glass of arak is consumed, a sort of cheers that carries respect and dignity.

Ghraybeh
Shortbread biscuit

makes 50

vegetable oil, for greasing, optional
300 g (10½ oz) unsalted butter, softened
110 g (3¾ oz/½ cup) sugar
500 g (1 lb 2 oz/3⅓ cups) plain (all-purpose) flour, sifted
65 g (2½ oz/heaped ½ cup) fine semolina, sifted
1–2 tablespoons warm milk
80 g (2¾ oz/½ cup) blanched almonds, halved

Preheat the oven to 150°C (300°F/Gas 2). Grease baking trays with oil or line with baking paper.

Beat the butter and sugar until fluffy. Add the flour, semolina and 1 tablespoon of the milk. Knead the mixture by hand until soft. If the mixture looks too soft, add a little flour; if it looks too firm, add the rest of the milk.

Lightly sprinkle flour on a work surface and roll 1 tablespoon amounts of dough into a sausage about 5 mm (¼ inch) thick. Join the ends of the length of dough to make a ring. Transfer to the baking tray. Place an almond at the join. Repeat with the rest of the dough and almonds. Bake for 30 minutes.

Gateau jazar
Carrot cake

serves 10

250 ml (9 fl oz/1 cup) vegetable oil, plus extra, for greasing
100 g (3½ oz/1 cup) walnuts
260 g (9¼ oz/2 cups) grated carrot
300 g (10½ oz/2 cups) plain (all-purpose) flour, sifted
4 eggs
330 g (11½ oz/1½ cups) white sugar
1½ teaspoons baking powder
125 g (4½ oz/1 cup) sultanas
icing (confectioners') sugar, for dusting

Preheat the oven to 170°C (325°F/Gas 3). Grease a 27 cm (10 inch) round cake tin and line with baking paper.

Place the walnuts in a food processor and pulse until chopped. Place in a large bowl with the carrot, flour, eggs, oil, white sugar, baking powder and sultanas. Mix together using one hand as a whisk (it is a good idea to wear a glove) for 5 minutes. Spoon into the prepared tin. Bake for 45 minutes, or until light golden and a skewer inserted into the centre comes out clean.

Cool completely in the tin. Remove from the tin, dust with icing sugar and serve.

Macaroni bil atter
Macaroni in sugar

serves 12

There is no macaroni in this recipe—I think it got its name because it is supposed to look like macaroni. This is Mum's favourite sweet.

2 teaspoons orange blossom water

2 quantities sugar syrup, at room temperature (see page 222)

550 g (1 lb 4 oz) coarse semolina, sifted

150 g (5½ oz/1 cup) self-raising (self-rising) flour, sifted, plus extra, for dusting

250 g (9 oz) unsalted butter, softened

½ teaspoon mahlab (aromatic spice, see page 22)

300 ml (10½ fl oz) milk

1 litre (35 fl oz/4 cups) vegetable oil, for deep-frying

Stir the orange blossom water into the sugar syrup and set aside until needed.

Combine the semolina, flour, butter, mahlab and milk in a bowl. Mix well, then knead until you have a soft even consistency, dusting your hands with flour as you knead. Roll 1 tablespoon of the mixture between your palms into a ball. Roll the ball out into a sausage about 1 cm (½ inch) thick. Hold the 'sausage' in one palm and, using your other hand, make deep imprints with the tips of four fingers along its length. Set aside. Repeat with the remaining dough until it is all used.

Heat the oil in a deep saucepan to 160°C (315°F). Fry the dough pieces in batches for 4–5 minutes, or until slightly golden brown. Remove the 'macaroni' from the oil and drain on kitchen paper. Place the 'macaroni' in a bowl and drench with the syrup.

Note: If you like, press the dough 'sausages' against the side of a sieve to add a pattern.

Barozee

Sesame biscuits

makes 24

vegetable oil, for greasing, optional
1 eggwhite
80 g (2¾ oz/½ cup) sesame seeds
675 g (1 lb 8 oz/4½ cups) self-raising (self-rising) flour, sifted
90 g (3¼ oz/¾ cup) icing (confectioners') sugar, sifted
125 ml (4 fl oz/½ cup) milk
pinch of mahlab (aromatic spice, see page 22)
250 g (9 oz) unsalted butter, melted and cooled

Preheat the oven to 200°C (400°F/Gas 6). Grease three baking trays with oil or line with baking paper.

Whisk the eggwhite in a bowl. Place the sesame seeds in a wide, shallow bowl. Set both aside until needed.

In a separate large bowl, mix the flour, icing sugar, milk, mahlab and butter together until you have a dough-like consistency. Knead the dough until it is soft and smooth. Roll one-quarter of the dough out to 1.5 cm (⅝ inch) thick. Cut out circles 8 cm (3¼ inches) in diameter. Brush the top of the circles with the eggwhite, then gently press into the sesame seeds. Put the discs on the baking trays. Using your fingers gently press the seeds down. Bake for 15–20 minutes, until they become slightly golden. Repeat with the remaining dough, re-rolling the offcuts.

Mulbeeyeah
Rice pudding

serves 8

1.5 litres (52 fl oz/6 cups) milk

165 g (5¾ oz/⅔ cup) sugar

440 g (15½ oz/2 cups) medium-grain rice, well washed

1 bay leaf

ground cinnamon, powdered chocolate or chocolate sprinkles, for garnish

Place the milk, 125 ml (4 fl oz/½ cup) of water and the sugar in a saucepan over high heat and bring to the boil. Add the rice and bay leaf and stir while bringing back to the boil. Reduce the heat to as low as possible, partially cover with a lid and simmer for 30–40 minutes, or until the rice pudding thickens.

Place the rice pudding in dessert bowls. Sprinkle with ground cinnamon, powdered chocolate or chocolate sprinkles.

Knefeh ma'a jubn
Knefeh with cheese

serves 10

vegetable oil, for greasing

625 ml (21½ fl oz/2½ cups) milk

220 g (7¾ oz/1 cup) sugar

240 g (8½ oz/1½ cups) coarse semolina

1 teaspoon rosewater or orange blossom water

125 g (4½ oz/1 cup) shredded mozzarella cheese

½ quantity sugar syrup, at room temperature (see page 222)

Preheat the oven to 180°C (350°F/Gas 4). Grease a 25 cm (10 inch) round cake tin.

Combine the milk, sugar, semolina, rosewater and 250 ml (9 fl oz/1 cup) of water in a saucepan over medium heat. Stir constantly for 20–30 minutes, or until it boils and thickens to a creamy consistency.

Pour half of the creamy semolina into the prepared tin. Sprinkle with cheese to cover. Add the remaining semolina and spread out evenly.

Bake for 25 minutes or until lightly coloured. Remove from the oven and allow to cool slightly. Cut into wedges and serve with sugar syrup.

Knefeh

Semolina cake with cornflake crumbs

serves 10

20 g (¾ oz) unsalted butter, chopped

30 g (1 oz) cornflakes, crushed

1 litre (35 fl oz/4 cups) milk

160 g (5¾ oz/1 cup) coarse semolina

250 ml (9 fl oz/1 cup) cream

1 tablespoon sugar

1 quantity sugar syrup, at room temperature (see page 222)

Preheat the oven to 180°C (350°F/Gas 4). Put the butter and cornflake crumbs in a flameproof round baking dish that is about 30 cm (12 inches) in diameter and 5 cm (2 inches) deep. Place the dish on the stovetop over medium–low heat and cook until the butter melts, stirring so the crumbs don't burn.

Divide the crumb mixture into two portions. Spread half of the crumbs in a thin layer to cover the base of the baking dish.

Combine the milk, semolina, cream and sugar in a saucepan. Stir over high heat until it boils and thickens. Reduce the heat to low and continue to cook, stirring often, for 10 minutes, or until thick.

Pour the creamy semolina mixture over the crumb mixture, level it and cover the top with the remainder of the crumb mixture. Bake for 15–20 minutes, or until the crumbs turn a caramel colour.

Remove from the oven and allow to rest for 10–20 minutes to cool down. Cut into wedges and serve with the syrup.

Hulwet jubneh
Sweet cheese

serves 12

This recipe requires continuous stirring during the entire cooking process. Think of it as working off the calories before you treat yourself.

Syrup
110 g (3¾ oz/½ cup) sugar
juice of ½ lemon, strained

Cheese
440 g (15½ oz/2 cups) sugar
1 kg (2 lb 4 oz) mozzarella cheese, cubed
270–360 g (9½–12¾ oz/1½–2 cups) fine semolina
4 tablespoons rosewater or orange blossom water

40 g (1½ oz/⅓ cup) crushed pistachio kernels

For the syrup, put the sugar, lemon juice and 4 tablespoons of water in a small saucepan over low heat, stirring to dissolve the sugar. Once the sugar is dissolved, stop stirring, increase the heat to high and bring to the boil. Reduce the heat to low and simmer for 6 minutes, or until syrupy. Set aside to cool.

For the cheese, put the sugar and 500 ml (17 fl oz/2 cups) of water in a non-stick saucepan over high heat and keep stirring until the sugar dissolves and the water boils. Add the cheese cubes, a little at a time, and slowly stir upwards in a circular motion. Slowly pour in small quantities of the semolina (reserving some), while continuing to stir. The cheese should get stringy. The cheese might not need all of the semolina—you can stop adding the semolina once there is no more water and the cheese becomes very thick. Add the rosewater and stir well.

Pour some of the cooled syrup onto a work surface and roughly spread over a 60 × 60 cm (24 × 24 inch) area. Roughly spread the cheese over the syrup to about 3 mm (⅛ inch) thick.

Allow to cool for 5 minutes, then tear rough 10 cm (4 inch) long pieces of the sweet cheese and place on a platter, layering them on top of each other. Sprinkle the sweet cheese with the crushed pistachios and some of the remaining syrup.

Note: This is delicious served with ashta, Lebanese clotted cream, available from Lebanese grocers.

Namoora

Baked semolina slice

makes 30

95 g (3¼ oz) unsalted butter, chopped

¾ teaspoon active dry yeast

750 g (1 lb 10 oz/4⅔ cups) coarse semolina

135 g (4¾ oz/1½ cups) desiccated coconut

330 g (11½ oz/1½ cups) white sugar

50 g (1¾ oz) blanched almonds, halved

Syrup

345 g (12 oz/1½ cups) caster (superfine) sugar

3 teaspoons lemon juice

3 small thin pieces of lemon rind, pith removed

Melt the butter in a small saucepan over low heat. Set aside to cool slightly. Place the yeast in a small bowl and combine with 3 teaspoons of lukewarm water.

Combine the semolina, coconut, sugar and 185 ml (6 fl oz/ ¾ cup) of water in a large bowl. Add the melted butter and the yeast mixture. Mix together and scrunch the mixture using your hands until you have a sticky mixture that holds together in a big ball.

Press the mixture into a 33 cm (13 inch) round cake tin that is about 5 cm (2 inches) deep. Cut into diamond shapes 3.5 × 5.5 cm (1¼ x 2¼ inches). Firmly press an almond half into the middle of each piece. Cover with plastic wrap and set aside to rest for 3 hours.

After 1½ hours, make the syrup. Place the sugar, lemon juice and rind and 270 ml (9½ fl oz) of water in a small saucepan over low heat, stirring to dissolve the sugar. Once the sugar is dissolved, stop stirring, increase the heat to high and bring to the boil. Reduce the heat to low and simmer for 8 minutes, or until slightly syrupy. The syrup is ready once the lemon rind is translucent and starting to curl at the edges. Remove from the heat and set aside to cool to room temperature. Remove the rind.

Preheat the oven to 180°C (350°F/Gas 4), remove the plastic wrap from the namoora and bake the cake for 40 minutes, or until the top is golden brown.

Remove from the oven. Turn the oven off. Pour the syrup over the cake. Return to the oven, close the door and leave for 15 minutes (the oven will be warm enough to allow the cake to absorb the syrup). Remove from the oven and allow to cool completely. Cut into pieces.

Murabba it tin

Fig and nut jam

makes 6½ cups

1 kg (2 lb 4 oz) dried figs

230 g (8 oz/1 cup) caster (superfine) sugar

100 g (3½ oz/1 cup) walnuts, roughly chopped

160 g (5¾ oz/1 cup) peanuts, skins removed, toasted

155 g (5¾ oz/1 cup) toasted sesame seeds (available from Lebanese grocers, or toast your own)

1 teaspoon rosewater

Remove the stems from the figs. Halve the figs lengthways and cut into thin slices.

Put the figs, sugar and 1 litre (35 fl oz/4 cups) of water into a large saucepan. Bring to the boil over low heat, stirring occasionally. Reduce the heat to very low or use a simmer pad. Cover and cook for 25 minutes, or until the figs start to soften. Add the nuts and sesame seeds and cook, covered, for 30 minutes. Uncover and cook for a further 20 minutes, or until thick, stirring and watching carefully until all the moisture has evaporated. Stir in the rosewater. Allow to cool slightly and store in sterilised glass jars in the fridge.

Murabba il mish mish

Apricot jam

makes 2¼ cups

Mum likes to mix very ripe apricots with semi-ripe apricots for a tart taste.

1 kg (2 lb 4 oz) apricots

1 bay leaf

220 g (7¾ oz/1 cup) raw sugar

Wash the apricots and remove any stems. Rip or cut open the apricots and remove the stones.

Place the apricots in a saucepan with 170 ml (5½ fl oz/⅔ cup) of water, the bay leaf and sugar. Mix together and bring to the boil over medium heat. Reduce the heat to very low or use a simmer pad. Simmer, stirring occasionally, for 1 hour. After 1 hour, if the jam is not thick enough, continue cooking until a thick consistency. The colour should be dark, rich honeycomb. Remove from the heat and pour into a heatproof bowl to cool slightly. Once the jam has cooled, transfer to sterilised glass jars. Store in the fridge.

Ahweh / Lebanese coffee

serves 6

'The golden rule is to make sure that the coffee sits aside to settle for 2 minutes.' Aunty Therese

When serving coffee for funerals, it is traditional to omit the sugar.

2 teaspoons sugar
4 teaspoons finely ground Lebanese
   coffee

In a small rakweh (narrow long-handled pot), boil 375 ml (13 fl oz/1½ cups) of water over medium heat. Once the water begins to boil, add the sugar. Remove the rakweh from the heat, add the coffee and stir. Reduce the heat to low and return the rakweh to the heat. Watch the coffee as it simmers. The foam should turn into bubbles. Remove from the heat once it stops forming froth or bubbles. Cover the rakweh with a small plate to settle for about 2 minutes. Serve in demitasse cups.

Cafe blanc / Digestive Lebanese tea

serves 1

1 teaspoon rosewater or orange
   blossom water
sugar, to serve, optional

Boil 250 ml (9 fl oz/1 cup) of water. Pour into a teacup and add the rosewater or orange blossom water. Add sugar, if you like.

Yensoon / Aniseed Tea

serves 1

1 teaspoon whole aniseed

Boil 250 ml (9 fl oz/1 cup) of water. Pour into a teacup. Wash the aniseed in a small sieve. Place in a tea strainer and place in the teacup. The longer you leave it to infuse, the stronger the flavour of the tea.

Published in 2011 by Murdoch Books Pty Limited

Murdoch Books Australia
Pier 8/9
23 Hickson Road
Millers Point NSW 2000
Phone: +61 (0) 2 8220 2000
Fax: +61 (0) 2 8220 2558
www.murdochbooks.com.au

Murdoch Books UK Limited
Erico House, 6th Floor
93–99 Upper Richmond Road
Putney, London SW15 2TG
Phone: +44 (0) 20 8785 5995
Fax: +44 (0) 20 8785 5985
www.murdochbooks.co.uk

Publisher: Kylie Walker
Project Manager: Livia Caiazzo
Photographer: Johan Palsson
Stylist: Mary Harris
Designer: Emilia Toia
Editor: Zoe Harpham
Food Consultant: Sonia Greig
Production Controller: Alexandra Gonzalez

National Library of Australia Cataloguing-in-Publication Data

Author: Taouk, Nouha.
Title: Whispers from a Lebanese kitchen / Nouha Taouk.
ISBN: 978-1-74196-822-4 (hbk.)
Notes: Includes index.
Subjects: Cooking, Lebanese.
Lebanese Australians--Social life and customs.

Dewey Number: 641.595692

A catalogue record for this book is available from the British Library.

Printed by 1010 Printing International Limited, China

IMPORTANT: Those who might be at risk from the effects of salmonella poisoning
(the elderly, pregnant women, young children and those suffering from immune
deficiency diseases) should consult their doctor with any concerns about eating
raw eggs.

OVEN GUIDE: You may find cooking times vary depending on the oven you are
using. For fan-forced ovens, as a general rule, set the oven temperature to 20°C
(35°F) lower than indicated in the recipe.